THE OPTIMISM CODE

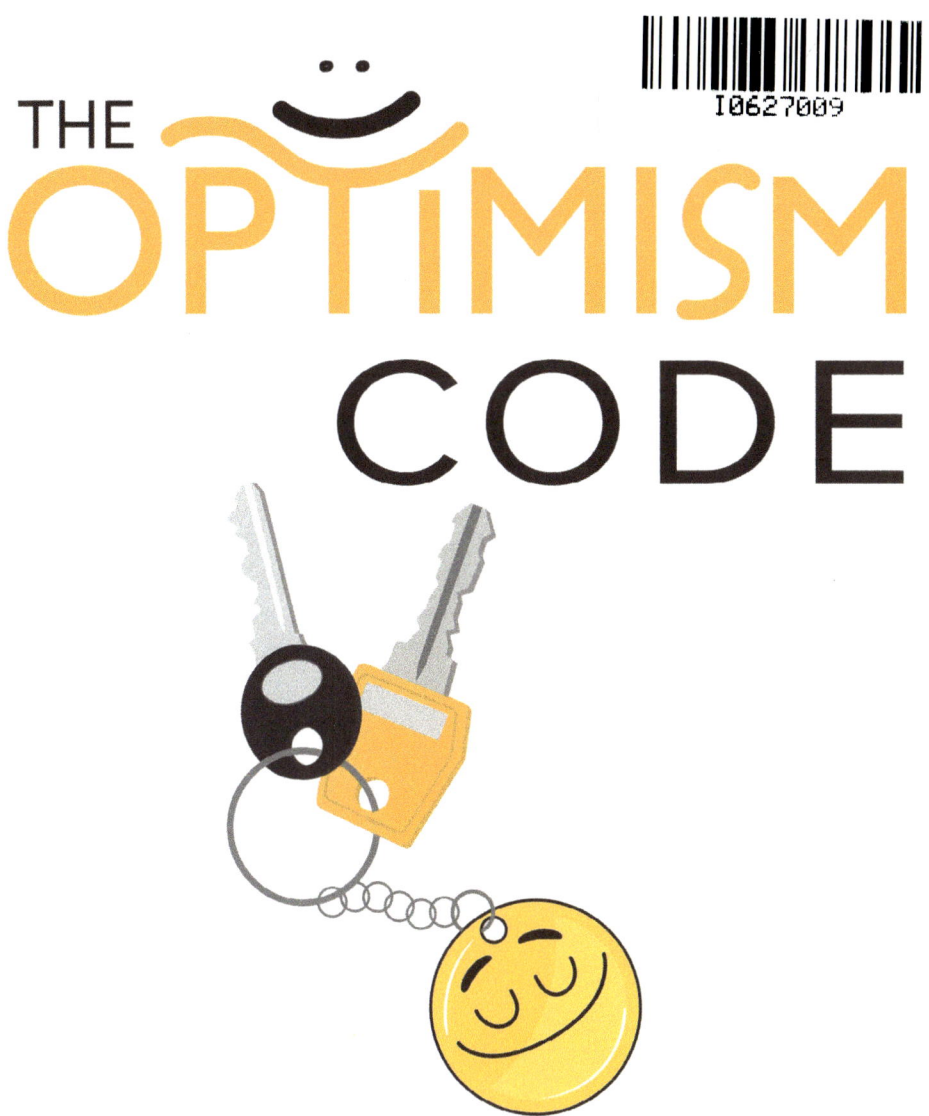

Grab the Keys to
Unlock Your Best Self

WENDY J. SCHWARTZ

Published by The Optimism Code LLC
www.theoptimismcode.com

Hardback ISBN-13: 979-8-9919506-1-9

Paperback ISBN-13: 979-8-9919506-0-2

eBook ISBN-13: 979-8-9919506-1-9

Library of Congress Control Number: 2024923642

DISCLAIMER

The Optimism Code: Grab the Keys to Unlock Your Best Self is intended to aid emotionally sensitive people in achieving greater levels of life satisfaction through a variety of self-help strategies. The information provided by the Optimism Code LLC and Wendy J. Schwartz is for educational purposes only and is not intended as a substitute for seeking help from a licensed healthcare professional and/or medical provider. We assume no legal liability for results or actions taken regarding use or non-use of this educational information.

The client examples in this book are fictionalized composites for the purposes of illustration. In addition, any content in this writing that is not cited appropriately or bears similarities to other creators is not an intentional act. Should any creator have an issue with anything published by the Optimism Code LLC, please address all concerns to info@optimismcode.com.

For more information, scan QR Code
or enter URL link into any browser.

https://theoptimismcode.com

ACKNOWLEDGEMENTS

"No one who achieves success does so without the help of others, the wise and confident acknowledge this help with gratitude."

Alfred North Whitehead

I am extremely grateful for the support I received from so many people throughout the creation of this book. In particular, I would like to mention the following individuals who inspired and motivated me along the way to achieve this monumental goal.

Special Thanks!

Kevin Wilhelm, Dinah Laprairie, Deborah Schoenbaum, Kevin Walker, D.M. Prior, Marcy Pusey, Lisa Chance, Terri Lance, Jamie Cipriani, Heather Shuker, and the coaching team at The Fasting Method

TABLE OF CONTENTS

Refute negative thoughts with ease. Learn a quick and effective method that uses slogans and clichés to replace counterproductive thinking instantly. Combat that hard-wired thinking driving your stress and anxiety.

INTRODUCTION

"Optimism is the faith that leads to achievement. Nothing can be done without hope and confidence."

Helen Keller

Have you struggled with stress and anxiety? I know I sure have. Do negative thoughts and feelings interfere with your life like an unwelcome intruder? Me too. If you have tried other self-help methods and are still feeling less than optimistic about life, welcome to *The Optimism Code: Grab the Keys to Unlock Your Best Self*.

I have learned that approximately 20% of the population are emotionally sensitive. That is one in five people. It was a relief to know I wasn't alone. I was determined to have a better life and to be my best self, so I set out on a journey of transformation.

Through trial and error, I unlocked what worked and what didn't, developing a series of strategies that slowly but surely boosted my positivity. Whether you were born anxious or became that way as a result of your life experiences, *The Optimism Code: Grab the Keys to Unlock Your Best Self* will guide you as you learn the simple secrets to overcoming life's daily challenges in a way that brings you greater happiness than you ever thought possible.

WHO THIS BOOK IS FOR

If you have been labeled sensitive because you have strong emotions, feel frequently stressed and anxious, have juggled overwhelming responsibilities, or suffer from chronic illness, this book is for you. Even if all you want is a more joyful existence, the methods I share here, gathered over many years of research, have been tweaked to offer maximum benefit in the least amount of time possible. As you increase your positivity, you will get the added bonus of becoming more productive and satisfied.

The Optimism Code: Grab the Keys to Unlock Your Best Self melds together easy-to-implement techniques that efficiently direct you toward greater levels of well-being. Throughout this journey, you will learn how to adopt simple strategies, transforming yourself from frustrated and upset to more optimistic than you ever thought imaginable. In the following chapters, I will be your guide, sharing stories about my own quest for optimism to encourage you on your unique path toward assembling a personal optimism keychain.

WHAT THIS BOOK ISN'T

This book won't solve all your problems, although that does sound wonderful. It also won't focus on the vast amounts of research related to the benefits of optimism in general. Instead, we will zero in on the "how-to" steps of improving life, even when it's imperfect. As you go through each chapter, I will share simple ways to reverse pessimistic thinking that may slowly and methodically rob you of maximum joy.

Starting from Chapter 1, you will begin assembling a sturdy set of keys to unlock more optimism, easing your mind in new ways. While you may be familiar with some of the methods used in this book, I feel sure you will learn many new techniques and gain valuable insights as you put it all together in a unique, more effective way.

Your road to success begins with gaining a better understanding of how the brain organizes thoughts and processes life events. You will get a glimpse at why it's so easy to spiral into a state of worry. While I have organized this book so that you can skip chapters if you would like to, I recommend reading it from start to finish to get the most out of it.

WHAT WE WILL COVER

Gratitude

Once you have a better understanding of how your brain thinks, we will explore the benefits of gratitude. Gratitude is one of the quickest, most powerful methods to achieve a positive outlook on life, especially when things aren't going exactly as planned. I will share easy steps to help you shift focus instantly toward the positive, leveraging your new gratitude habit. If you already have a consistent gratitude routine, this chapter will reinforce it and give you new insight.

Non-Meditation Mindfulness (NMM)

We will go on a deep dive into one of my absolute favorite set of keys, focusing on "easy-to-adopt" approaches to mindfulness that don't require you to meditate. So many people have told me that they find it nearly impossible to meditate when their "monkey mind" is active. For this very reason, I created this special chapter with some of the easiest mindfulness hacks on the planet. By the time you are done reading about NMMs, you will have new tools you can use at work or home to transform you from discouraged to empowered, often in seconds.

TOC Talk — Unique Self Talk Strategies

After exploring gratitude and non-meditation mindfulness, you will be ready to delve into TOC Talk. TOC is an acronym for The Optimism Code and self-talk is all about what you choose to say when you "speak" to yourself. We all have that underlying, oftentimes unwelcome, voice that says seemingly counterproductive things. TOC Talk will be your new "go-to language" so you can redirect your brain.

Learning to communicate with yourself in a new way is easy and fun once you understand your brain's true goals. As you practice self-optimism skills, you will gain mastery at taming unwieldy negative thoughts. By adopting key phrases, clichés, and affirmations, and understanding the basics of what I call "re-framers," you will begin to speak nicely to yourself with a new language designed to promote peace of mind.

More Traditional Meditation

I have also included a broad overview of the various methods used to practice meditation. I encourage you to consider experimenting. Many who at first resisted meditation have found that once they mastered the non-meditation mindfulness techniques in combination with more gratitude and TOC Talk, classic meditation became much easier.

Meditation has the power to help you develop a calmer, more balanced mind. I love meditation and get some of my most creative ideas when my mind quiets down. If you have tried meditation in the past and think of it as an epic fail, you will want to read this chapter. If you already meditate regularly, you will hopefully learn a few new methods.

Healthy Brain Tips

In addition to exploring the various keys you can use to boost your optimism, I will share some secrets I have learned for optimizing health habits. By focusing on nutrition, supplementation, fitness, adequate rest, and self-care, you can boost optimism even more. In addition to my passion for optimism, I am passionate about nutrition and physical fitness, and will provide simple hacks designed to improve your mind by caring for your body.

Assembling Your Keys

Lastly, you will be able to review the various keys and combine your own sequences to create an optimism keychain designed to boost your mood daily for long-lasting results.

My "why" for writing this book is that it worked for me, and it can work for you too. The many programs I have participated in over the years have molded me and led to my own transformation. Is my life perfect? Am I perfect? Absolutely not, but I do my best to return to an outlook that brings me joy every single day, and that is truly priceless. I have more happiness than I ever thought possible. I am excited to share what I have learned in a fun and easy way so you can make the most out of your life, too.

What will your life look like a week, month, or year from now if you don't adopt better ways to boost your mood? Can you really continue to live in a state of sub-optimism? Wouldn't you rather create a life filled with hopeful anticipation and positivity? I hope you will join me on my mission to help people, including you, to unlock more joy. You're in charge, so grab the keys and read on!

Chapter 1

Starting Your Journey Down the Road to Optimism

"Optimism is the faith that leads to achievement. Nothing can be done without hope and confidence."

Helen Keller

Seeing is Believing

I nearly went blind! It was scary. Really scary.

Luckily for me, it was only my left eye. Nevertheless, it was still very frightening to potentially lose my sight. Suddenly, I found myself lying on one side, unable to work for weeks while my eye healed. I waited, not-so-patiently, as the gas bubble that had been injected into the center as a protective measure dissipated.

I had a lot of time to think as I healed, and I wondered how this would impact my income, my life, and my joy. When the bubble was finally gone, a squiggly brown inchworm of a floater I nicknamed the "squirmy worm" appeared in my vision. Unfortunately, it still hasn't gone away and may never leave. It likes to swirl around as if it has a mind of its own. On cloudy days, it reminds me of a windshield wiper moving back and forth in my field of vision.

The eye specialist told me maybe, just maybe, if and when I get cataract surgery, which could be 15 years from now, I might be able to remove it. He sounded very iffy. Despite the "squirmy worm" remaining, I am abundantly grateful and consider myself very fortunate. It could have been so much worse.

The former pessimistic me would likely have reacted differently. I doubt I would have taken the news that the "squirmy worm" was here to stay very well. While I wasn't thrilled and it took me a while to adapt, my past self might have cried my eyes out repeatedly, which I'm sure would not have helped my detached retina to heal. I may have even blamed the eye surgeon or spiraled into self-blame, chastising myself for not getting it checked out sooner. Pessimistic me would have given myself a bad case of the self-pity blues.

I remember my inner thoughts at the time:

Why didn't I go to the doctor sooner?

Is this "squirmy worm" really gonna be in my eye for the rest of my life?

I can't deal with this.

Did the doctor do something wrong?

Did I cause this with my mascara?

What am I gonna do now?

That non-stop voice! The incessant chatter even had my New York accent.

Depending upon the circumstances, my "monkey mind" told me different things, often repeating similar themes of doom and gloom. I am guessing you know exactly what I'm talking about if you sometimes hear that voice, too. It gets noisy in there, doesn't it? Whether your inner voice is loud, or hiding subtly in the background, it probably says things that are seemingly spontaneous and uncontrollable. The good news is that managing and redirecting that voice rather than picking on it, or trying to quash it, is a learnable skill.

Getting back to the "squirmy worm" story, even though I can't see perfectly, my vision could be so much worse, and I am thrilled for the vision I have. As a person committed to living in a state of optimism, I choose to focus (pardon the pun) on the positives rather than dwell on the loss. Who knows? It's even possible this outcome is going to be better for me in some way that isn't necessarily apparent yet. What an optimistic thought!

I really could have gone blind, no exaggeration. The doctor was amazing, and I felt he really cared, which was nice. I truly believe he did the best he could under the circumstances. One of the special things that came out of this experience, in addition to meeting some really great people along the way, was the awareness that I am no longer the miserable me of the past. Another positive was that I had the opportunity to witness people who love me helping out in a crisis. That was a priceless outcome for me.

I share this story to illustrate the value of seeking a positive viewpoint when things aren't necessarily what you might consider positive. Emphasizing the good is far better, no matter what roadblocks you encounter in life. There have been Holocaust survivors, amputees, and abuse victims who have risen above what has happened to them using the power of optimism. Helen Keller was a woman with abundant optimism who persevered despite the challenges she faced. She is only one among many to overcome seemingly insurmountable obstacles.

If you are reading this with the skepticism of a pessimist, I understand. As someone who has always been sensitive, I wasn't always focused on a life of optimism. I had to cultivate optimism, and you can too. It's easier than you think. This does not mean you won't have a response to negative stimuli. We are all human and when the unexpected happens, it is sometimes not possible to avoid an immediate reaction.

Unhappy Camper

To provide contrast, I want to share a very different story and give you an idea of just how much a mindset of optimism can change life for the better. Sadly, I have way too many stories like this of living in a state of perpetual stress, anxiety, and disappointment. On the bright side, it was a good training ground for creating The Optimism Code.

When I was in my 20s, I had the opportunity to go to a small island in the Dutch Antilles on a dream vacation with friends. Upon arrival to our villa, I went out onto a spacious veranda with a panoramic view leading directly to the Caribbean sea. This would have been idyllic except the stairs into the water were as slimy as a scene from *Ghostbusters*. My feet slipped as I descended vertically, one slippery rung at a time, down a rusty metal ladder coated in what must have been greenish-brown algae. My toes clung unwillingly to the sea muck. I was not a happy camper, to say the least. I can't totally recall what I said to myself that day, but it went something like this:

What am I doing on this slimy ladder?

What was I thinking, coming to this island?

This place doesn't even have air conditioning!

And the bugs.

How am I gonna stay here for a week?

Get me outta here!

I wanna go home.

I was in paradise but acted like I was being slow-tortured. I whined and complained, focusing heavily on what was wrong. At that time, in my mind, everything had to be perfect, and when it wasn't, I was very good at turning molehills into mountains. I lived with disillusionment and frustration when the universe fell short of my expectations. I allowed myself to get overly upset about one thing or another nearly every hour on the hour.

Whether by nature, nurture, or a bit of both, I am still prone to that initial negative response when life unexpectedly disappoints me. I won't hide that from you because I want you to know this is normal for many, particularly for those of us who are on the sensitive side. Getting back to those slimy, mucky stairs, I regret that I didn't know how full my glass truly was at the time.

To this day, I vividly remember how incredible it was once I got to the bottom rung. It was the absolute best snorkeling I have ever experienced. There were colorful fish of all varieties within inches of my mask. A puffer fish even blew up right before my eyes. What an amazing experience. It's sad I wasn't able to enjoy it fully at the time.

I do want to cut myself a little slack though. Negativity can be a bit hardwired in the brain. The tendency to think the worst is a knee-jerk reaction, a natural instinct. The human brain (aka the "monkey mind") is constantly scanning for threats as a protective mechanism. It's important to recognize that there is nothing inherently wrong with you when your mind leans toward the negative. Just like a wild monkey, the mind needs taming. In the following pages, I will share how you can use specific keys to rapidly restore positivity and well-being in seconds and minutes rather than hours or days.

Pollyanna or Pragmatist?

Finding the good in life doesn't come naturally to me. Unlike Pollyanna, the fictional character who always sees the best in everything, I adopted optimism because I decided that living a life fraught with anxiety was no fun. It was a pragmatic decision based on the fact that I didn't want to spend time wallowing in misery.

I have learned to work with my initial pessimistic reactions in a way that minimizes my upset and maximizes my happiness. Let's face it. Life is never going to be 100% easy for any of us, no matter how hard we try to make it that way. The freedom that comes from knowing how to transform your own thinking, sooner rather than later, is nothing short of a miracle.

My goal is not to fake it and pretend everything is wonderful. I couldn't be a Pollyanna if I tried. Instead, I focus on using the best strategies (keys) on my personal optimism keychain to transform and unlock the positives as quickly as possible. Sometimes, it requires a moment of gratitude for all the good I have. At other times, positive self-talk works. Refocusing my attention elsewhere is yet another way I get over unpleasant situations quickly. Determining the best keys to get me back to my happy place is what it's all about.

Why The Optimism Code?

I wanted to write this book because gathering the keys that unlocked me from my shackles has had a profound impact on my life. I felt I couldn't possibly keep this information all to myself. While I am still a work in progress in many ways, I am honored to share the keys I have developed with you.

Within these pages, I will lay out a unique, multi-pronged approach that borrows from the best in positive psychology and simplifies things for busy people who prefer an easy, natural approach to managing stress and anxiety. My goal is to cut through the noise and get down to what works.

Before going any further, I want to mention that this book is not a replacement for the role that professionals may play in your life. I am a writer and a coach. As mentioned in the disclaimer, this content is for educational purposes only, and *The Optimism Code: Grab the Keys to Unlock Your Best Self* is not intended to replace appropriate healthcare.

Which Keys Open Your Optimism Door?

In the coming chapters, I will take you on a voyage into the brain and teach you how to befriend your own mind. By gaining a more compassionate understanding of why you think, feel, and behave in seemingly counterproductive ways, you will learn the necessary skills to downplay and override much of your programming.

"I'm not good enough," "It must be something I'm doing wrong," or similar variations of negative self-talk are common. Sometimes, that judgmental voice may be subtle, lurking in the background, while other times you may hear yourself thinking as loudly as a howler monkey.

Whether or not you have had exposure to some of the self-help techniques in this book, you will learn new combinations using a fresh approach. As we move forward, it will be my role to serve as your guide, but you get to determine which keys to put on your new optimism keychain. No one but you can decide how to mix and match the various keys that unlock your best self.

Since this new set of keys will be of your own unique design, you will have the opportunity to "take the best and leave the rest" as you decide what will and won't work. There is absolutely nothing in this book you must do, so no guilt, please! Many self-help books provide a one-size-fits-all approach that may not work for everyone.

To use the key analogy, what if you were to pick up the wrong set of keys by accident and arrive home only to realize you couldn't unlock the doors to your house? If you grab the keys to your best friend's house, they will do you no good. Once you understand which keys unlock maximum optimism for you and you alone, you will be able to assemble various key rings to create a custom keychain available only to you. Once you identify your favorite keys, you will easily unlock a better mindset.

Who Moved My Keys?

While you can skim through this book, I recommend exploring the content fully. This way, you will at least be aware of strategies you may want to implement down the line as you create your personal optimism keychain. For now, the most important thing to do is make it to the next page. One of my favorite clichés is "You never fail until you stop trying."

What Lies Ahead

In the following chapters, I will show you how to transform yourself from "woe is me" thinking to strategic optimism, using your brain's tendencies to your advantage. You will gain insight into how gratitude over the simple things in life can feed and nourish you. Together, we will explore a myriad of methods to ensure you are grateful, even on days that challenge you. You will also learn how to be present without meditating, gaining mastery at switching gears away from worry and upset to a more positive state of mind.

After exploring some of the easier non-meditation methods that are part of the Optimism Code, we will review easy-to-use slogans, clichés, affirmations, and reframing techniques. It is worth noting that you can turn things around by creating a new inner dialogue without necessarily erasing hardwired thought patterns. For now, let's get going on Chapter 2, and I will share more about why your brain is just doing its "brain thing" and not intentionally trying to sabotage you.

OPTIMISM DECODER

Chapter 1
Starting Your Journey Down The Road to Optimism

- You are capable of shifting your mindset from stress and anxiety to optimism using easy-to-learn keys.

- Life is likely never going to be perfect, so it's up to you to make a choice to live as your best self.

- There are many different techniques for boosting optimism and there is no one-size-fits-all approach. You are unique.

- Even if you are pessimistic by nature, this is not necessarily a bad thing. You can overcome negativity.

- It is not hard to cultivate optimism once you learn how.

https://theoptimismcode.com

Chapter 2

This is Your Brain on Optimism

"At the end of the day, we can endure much more than we think we can."

Frida Kahlo

Best Possible Outcome

I thought of myself as a mess, but the counselor I went to told me I was strong. Who knew? I didn't feel strong at the time, but in the end, I chose to believe her. I was going through a rough breakup at the time. Little did I know it would be a wonderful growth opportunity. I was spared from a relationship with the wrong person. Yay! In retrospect, I'm so grateful. It is in those moments when life feels less than pleasant that it's easy to miss the positive. What is happening, while temporarily painful, may be the best possible outcome in the long run.

From that day forward, I started to believe in myself more. Having a trained professional refer to me as strong when I felt like I was falling apart was very empowering. I had labeled myself weak because that was what I was told as an emotionally sensitive person. I bought into this faulty thinking. My brain believed it, even though it wasn't true. I didn't know I could see myself through a different lens.

I wasn't weak after all. I was just human with a little more sensitivity than others. I rebranded myself as quirky rather than fatally flawed. In time, my brain stopped repeating the scripts it had learned early in life that kept me loathing myself. I gradually reframed my thoughts and behaviors in a new, more positive light.

As I think back on the breakup that spurred me to go to counseling in the first place, I am so grateful I dodged that bullet. My heartache is long gone, and life unfolded much better than I could have imagined. I know firsthand it's hard to have perspective when you're going through the fire, but taking a position that you are strong is one of the first keys you can use as you begin to boost your optimism level.

🔑 TOC Key: I'm Just Human

I'm stronger than I think (even though I'm imperfect).

Acronym TOC = The Optimism Code

Your Amazing Brain

Our brains are very complex with many different functions, and if you want to understand more of the nitty-gritty, there are lots of great resources online on brain anatomy. Your brain is always on, doing its job to keep you alive and well. By retraining your brain to automatically seek optimism using the various TOC Keys, you will learn how to leverage your brain's superpowers in a positive way.

While the brain is really amazing, your thoughts and feelings can be counterproductive at times. The great news is that your brain can also be used to boost happiness. While you may not always be able to change what happened or even what is happening, you almost always have the option of shifting your mind and taking action to feel better.

Using Your Brain

Think of your brain as a "master protector" always looking out for you with underlying good intentions. However, in its fallibility, it can misinterpret situations, either overreacting or underreacting. This is why building an optimism keychain to unlock positivity in a variety of situations is so powerful.

Throughout this book, you'll find TOC Keys like the one above. By the end of this book, you will learn to assess situations and choose the absolute best TOC Keys to help you feel better fast. Using a combination of memory, physiology, and practice, you will become your own expert at protecting yourself from harm more effectively. You will establish a new arsenal of strategies to shield and protect you from life's unanticipated challenges. You will develop a mindset of optimism that will carry you through the tough times.

Using the Keys

As a simple example to illustrate how you might use a few TOC Keys in a real-life situation, I recently went for a walk in the park. While I live in a relatively safe community, I brought some self-defense spray with me just in case. Better safe than sorry. In my early 20s, I was jumped on a subway train. Fortunately, nothing too bad happened, but as a result, I am still vigilant.

Someone was loitering near the picnic shelter, and from a distance, it looked like he had lots of personal belongings with him. I didn't get close enough to determine his intent, but I did tense up. My initial thought was to berate myself for overreacting since he turned out to be harmless, but instead, I thanked my brain for doing its job to keep me safe from a perceived threat.

Once I assessed the situation and determined he was not a threat, I felt safer and was free to consciously shift my attention. I immediately began to use my TOC Keys to shift my mood toward enjoyment. I focused on a beautiful blue jay, a white egret, the sound of doves in the distance, and the fabulous views of the intracoastal waterway at the end of the pier. In other words, I enlisted my brain to go to work for me. It protected me based in the moment, which was great, but I wanted to quickly return to the present and enjoy my nature walk.

I used a number of TOC Keys to bring myself back to bliss. First, I took a nice, deep, slow breath in and out. Then, I recalled a couple of my favorite calming self-talk thoughts, *I'm safe, everything's gonna be all right.* Next, I intentionally shifted my attention, focusing on how grateful I was to see the birds and trees.

I even took the opportunity to tilt my head toward the warm morning sun on my way home for an added pleasure boost. The positive experience of getting out in nature and physically moving, combined with my use of a few TOC Keys, allowed my brain to relax in an instant, despite the unnerving startle.

This might seem like a relatively minor story, and in some ways it is. Still, if you were alone in a park and came across a stranger, there are several different ways you could react depending on your past experiences and temperament. Many people might not even notice the stranger. Some might decide to never walk alone in that park again. A few might even turn back and never visit the park ever again. Others might spend the entire walk unnerved and miss the opportunity to thoroughly enjoy the experience.

In this story, I had a choice to focus on the worst possible outcome and let it upset me, or shift gears and get as much positivity out of the moment as possible. Your perceived threat might be a work deadline, a sink full of dirty dishes that your spouse promised to clean, or a splitting headache that feels like it will never go away. Whatever the scenario, using a TOC Key or two can help you mitigate suffering and get on with life with as much joy as you can under the circumstances.

As I unpack ways you can pivot, you will learn about a wide array of TOC Keys that can be used at any given moment to switch gears toward the positive. In this example, I quickly focused on the birds after taking a deep breath. Once you know how to hack your brain in real-time, you can rapidly switch from fear and upset to joy.

Bodily Management

It's amazing to think about all of the wonderful things my brain does for me daily. All day, it directs my body, bringing nutrients via my blood to the places that need it most. I don't tell it what to do, yet it instructs my lungs to breathe vital oxygen in and out 24/7. It even heals me from paper cuts and infections.

The brain also sends alerts in a world filled with good and bad stimuli to let me know when I need to pay attention. These alerts impact bodily sensations and can be considered messengers. By recognizing our brain's primitive response, and using various TOC Keys, we can improve our bodily management.

Automation

In addition to managing all of your bodily functions on autopilot, the brain can put your thoughts and feelings on autopilot. Your thinking patterns and the behaviors you repeat daily are basically mini-programs or loops. The brain is designed for efficiency and attempts to simplify your life through automation.

This means that sometimes negative thinking can become a habit. The good news is that if you can automate negativity, you can just as easily automate positivity. Creating good messaging is as achievable as creating bad messaging. By leveraging your brain's natural tendencies, you can deliberately install new, empowering automation that, once memorized, will run with minimal effort.

Your Decision Maker

Your brain always wants to protect you, even when it seems like the opposite is true. Unfortunately, because your brain performs multiple functions, one part of your brain may not always be in full communication with the other. Think of a time when you wanted to lose weight but were confronted with chocolate cake. Learning to discern and listen to all parts of yourself is important. Having a game plan in advance for when that chocolate cake appears helps you make the right decision.

Your brain will "swing from the trees" to protect you. Is this good, or is this bad? Am I right or wrong? Is it safe or dangerous? Your brain constantly works to determine what's in your best interest and protect you from harm. I can't emphasize this point enough. As we set out to achieve our goals, one thing that often gets in the way is our interpretation of negative thoughts and feelings. We take them as true when they may or may not be. Just because your brain tells you something, this does not mean it is necessarily a fact.

To come back to the cake, you could think, *One little bite won't hurt*, or *I'm such a pig,* or *Sugar is not my friend.* You could even think about all three things in a matter of seconds. One part of your brain wants that delicious treat and another prefers to delay gratification. When you take your thoughts and feelings as being 100% factual, your brain is prone to misinterpretation. It's important to stop, assess, and adjust as necessary when making decisions.

Eating a piece of cake does not make you a pig, but if you are anything like me, one bite could lead you down a slippery slope. The choice is yours, and there isn't necessarily a right choice. Listening to the conflicting voices in your head and making the best decision for yourself gets easier as you boost your brain health while implementing the TOC Keys that work best for you.

Counterproductive Thinking

During the decision-making process, I can do a lot of what-ifs, counterproductive thinking. I like to call it "what-iffing." I know my brain has the goal of self-protection, but it can sometimes catastrophize unnecessarily, driving me into a state of overanalyzing things in a negative way. When I catch myself what-iffing, I use a simple TOC Key and think of three things that can go right in addition to looking at what might go wrong.

🔑 TOC Key: Positive What-Iffing

The next time you find yourself catastrophizing or ruminating about what might happen, ask yourself these questions:

"What good might come from this?"

"Is it possible the outcome could be a long-term win?"

"What if this turns out to be the best thing to happen?"

Let me share a brief example to further illustrate what I mean about what-iffing. I had a client who was job-seeking and worried that her interview might not go well. She had prepared for it and knew she was ready but was nervous. "What if I don't get the offer?" "What if I botch the interview?" "What if they don't pick me for next rounds?" These are all less than optimistic thoughts. Searching for a job can be highly stressful, particularly when income and career advancement are on the line. In her brain's effort to make predictions to protect her, it identified what could go wrong rather than what could go right. This was her brain's instinct kicking into survival mode.

I explained to her that if you think something bad might happen, you can just as easily think something good might happen once you learn to make it a habit. Together, she and I turned to the positive what-ifs of the situation that were missing from her initial thoughts. I said, "What if you do a great job? What if you get an offer that is exactly what you were hoping for? What if you don't get the role and an even better job is waiting right around the corner?"

After we explored a few positive what-ifs, she became much more optimistic, which helped her performance. She was more productive in preparing for the interview, and her optimistic attitude resulted in a solid offer. Happily, she wound up accepting another role from a competing firm. The TOC Key of positive what-iffing helped to calm her nerves, giving her hope of a positive outcome. As a result, she had two good interviews, not just one.

The original thoughts were still there as her brain strived to protect her, but she learned how to overwrite her initial natural response, taking charge of her mind. Hoping for the best with a spirit of optimism while you do what you can to prepare for the worst goes a long way toward cultivating peace of mind.

Interpretations Based on Context

Interpreting is another overlapping function of our brain. When you hear a siren blaring, you instantly decide if this is good or bad. Keep in mind that context matters. If you're waiting for an ambulance because a loved one is injured, the siren will be welcome, and you will likely feel relief when it arrives.

On the other hand, if you are having trouble falling asleep and the piercing sound of an ambulance stirs you, you are likely to become agitated and deem the siren a nuisance. Past life experiences can influence your interpretations significantly. When your brain filters information, you don't always get it right. This is important to remember as you build your set of TOC Keys to reframe some of your knee-jerk reactions.

Pleasure Seeking and Pain Avoidance

The brain, in making its decisions, is often focused on immediate pleasure seeking and pain avoidance, as illustrated by the chocolate cake story. What gives one person pleasure might cause another person pain. Weighing and balancing the pros and cons of pleasure-seeking and/or pain avoidance is an important skill to master. Blaming yourself is not helpful in cases where your monkey mind has hijacked you. Self-blame can lead to a bad case of the blues. By recognizing the natural tendency to gravitate toward pleasure and away from pain, you can reduce frustration, acknowledging that you are 'just human' when you fall short of your expectations for yourself!

Focus Shifts

One of the easiest ways to improve your mood immediately is with a quick focus shift. The great thing about changing focus is that most people have a good amount of control over where they direct their attention. If you have ever tried to entertain a toddler, you have used this method before. I want you to try a short, easy exercise before we move forward. I promise you're going to like it. It's simple and can be done whenever you focus on the negative.

🔑 TOC Key: The Sunshine Gaze

This simple key illustrates how quickly your state of mind can shift and how easy it is to refocus your attention. Whenever I do this exercise, it cheers me up instantly. It's an amazing example of how you can go from frustrated to feeling good in under 30 seconds.

- First, tilt your head as if looking up at the warm sun.

- Next, close your eyes and imagine putting your face toward the warm, soothing sunshine.

- You may have smiled naturally just thinking about it. But if not, smile and recall when the sun warmed your face.

- Hold this stance, take a big breath, and hold it for as long as comfortable.

- Slowly exhale!

How do you feel?

While a refocusing exercise like The Sunshine Gaze will not solve all your problems or transform you instantly into a happy-go-lucky person, it will shift your brain toward the positive, if only momentarily. I love practicing this and other TOC Keys to boost my mood instantly.

Judgment

I admit it. I am judgmental, as most of us are. Every single person interprets the world through a lens of judgment, so while some are more judgmental than others, this is not a defect. It is a built-in brain feature. Judgment is your mind's way of guiding you. It is a close cousin to discernment. Without judgment, you would not be the unique individual that you are.

For example, if I were raised in certain parts of Africa or Asia, I might wear rings to elongate my neck to be more beautiful. Because I was born in North America, it's not something I've ever desired to do, and I don't fully understand its cultural significance. However, wearing mascara to elongate my eyelashes is perfectly fine in my world. Are the neck rings wrong while the mascara is right?

In relationships at work and home, it is easy to take a polarized position, passing judgment on others whose viewpoints differ from ours. Do your best to catch yourself when making judgments from past programming that don't feel positive. While I have learned not to take my spontaneous judgmental thoughts too seriously (which we will discuss further) I strive to let go of judgments that make me feel agitated or upset.

As you assemble different key rings to create an optimism keychain all your own, I want you to use your brain's natural tendencies without judgment to aid you rather than hinder you. You will create pathways to spur new, more optimistic, automatic thoughts. In Chapter 3, we will explore one of the most effective ways to direct your attention toward more positive thought patterns: gratitude. Focusing on what you are grateful for daily is an amazing habit that opens the brain to amazing levels of optimism.

OPTIMISM DECODER

Chapter 2
This is Your Brain on Optimism

- Your brain is amazing and has a myriad of functions all designed to keep you well.

- Many of the things you do and say are programmed in and have become automatic.

- It's common for your brain to lean toward negative and judgmental thoughts in an effort to protect you.

- You can work with, rather than against, your brain to rapidly transform your thoughts and feelings.

https://theoptimismcode.com

Chapter 3

Becoming Grateful
For Nothing and Everything

"A successful life is built upon a foundation of being thankful for what you already have."

Bob Baker

Grateful for Gratitude

Sometimes, being grateful can be difficult in the face of adversity. If you're anything like me, you are regularly subjected to various challenges. Whether dealing with difficult people at work, family dynamics, wonky technology, time restraints, health ailments, or other "problems-du-jour," maintaining a "Gee, life is joyous" mindset isn't always easy. The stressors of everyday life can test our ability to remain cheery.

Focusing on gratitude allows you to be glad for what you have, even when life gets a little bumpy. I like to think of gratitude as my way of thanking the world for giving me abundance. If you are among the many people who regularly say grace or you've given thanks before a Thanksgiving dinner, then you are familiar with gratitude. You may have started a gratitude habit at some point and then let it fall by the wayside.

There are so many wonderful things to be grateful for that can easily be taken for granted. The excellent news about developing a habit of gratitude is that it's fairly easy to do. Even when your difficulties are more serious, adopting a gratitude practice can prevent you from wallowing in despair. If and when life dishes out highly stressful circumstances, turning your attention toward things you are grateful for is always better than focusing on negative situations that are seemingly out of your control.

In any given moment, you can use gratitude to direct your attention to the good in life while downplaying the not-so-good. Case in point: right now, as I write this, I have a lot of aches and pains. This is obviously not what I am grateful for. Who would be grateful for the pain? Yet, without our pain signals, we would be vulnerable to injury. What I *am* grateful for, aside from the brain's pain feedback system right now, is my super comfortable couch. I also appreciate my favorite pillows, which are propping me up. I'm also grateful my computer works so I can write this paragraph and share my story.

I don't want aches and pains, but they are already here, so now I have a choice. I can turn my attention toward what is wrong, or I can be grateful for what is right. My legs work today, and my hands are functioning. I have food, clothing, shelter, eyesight, and comfort items. If you are a *Survivor* fan like me, you know that comfort items are worth a lot when you're on a deserted island.

What Do You Have To Be Grateful For?

Focusing on what you are grateful for is easy and has the added benefit of conditioning your brain over time to notice even more positive things in your world that might have otherwise been overlooked. There are a variety of ways you can nurture gratitude in your life, and some are better than others, but I find the most important thing is to be consistent.

Even when you think there is absolutely nothing in your life you could be grateful for, you can always find something once you remember to look. On those rare days when I am less than enthusiastic about my life, I like to keep it simple with the following options:

1.   My hands work
2.   My eyes see
3.   I have air to breathe
4.   I have shelter
5.   I have food and water

Can you think of one thing you are grateful for at the moment?

_____

(You can write it down now or say it in your mind.)

If your hands or eyes don't work well, you can choose something that works properly for you today and be grateful for that instead. Nothing is too small or insignificant, especially if you are suffering with a case of the blues or experiencing physical discomfort of any sort.

Direct Your Attention

While you can't always control the thoughts that pop into your head or the circumstances life presents to you, you can direct your attention toward more positive thoughts. Gratitude allows you to intentionally dwell on what is working in your life for a quick boost of optimism. Being grateful for whatever you can think of at the moment gives you a burst of joy. You can be grateful for people, nature, running water, air conditioning, indoor plumbing, access to food, sunshine, butterflies, or pretty much anything you appreciate.

That said, gratitude is somewhat unique for each of us, so I don't recommend telling others what they should or shouldn't be grateful for unless you are pointing out possible suggestions like I did. Some people may be grateful for a great hard rock song, while others might love a twangy country tune. My father used to look out at the city skyline in awe, whereas I have always preferred the view at a scenic beach. The bottom line is that when you are busy focusing on your "haves," you will forget, if only for a moment, about your "have nots." No matter what else is going on in life, even on the darkest days, there is always something to be grateful for.

Starting Your Gratitude Habit

So, now that I have hopefully sold you on the benefits of gratitude, I want to discuss the how. The method I subscribe to allows you to choose what works best for you. If you have a cell phone, there's an app for that. If an app is not your thing, a piece of paper, a notepad (online or off), a journal, or even sticky notes will work. As an Android user, the app I have on my phone is called "Presently: A Gratitude Journal." It includes a daily inspirational quote, a lightbulb prompt to give you gratitude suggestions, and a blank space to jot down what you are grateful for in free form. You may want to download it.

There is an app called "Grateful: A Gratitude Journal" for iPhone users. I haven't used this particular one, however, it's worth noting that they cite Harvard Medical School research with the following statement, "Gratitude helps people feel more positive emotions, relish good experiences, improve their health, deal with adversity, and build strong relationships." Play around and see which apps you like best.

Stairway to Gratitude

I am going to share a "Good, Better, Best" approach to illustrate how you might make gratitude into a daily habit. As you decide which level of effort to choose, keep in mind that consistent small steps more easily form habits. This means that doing more, rather than less, could be counterproductive at first. Repetitive mini-actions are the key to developing habits, according to experts in habit formation. You may want to link your daily gratitude to something like morning coffee/tea or an evening ritual like washing your face before bed. This can help you automate your behavior as you create a new gratitude routine. I will share more about the technique of dovetailing in Chapter 9.

There is no shame in what I call the "quick and dirty" method, which I refer to as "good' in the TOC Key section below. In my opinion, doing the bare minimum daily is better than doing nothing at all. Once you develop a daily habit with your gratitude, you can always increase your efforts to the next level if this is helpful. Do what you feel works best, and don't be afraid to pivot. You want to do it daily or nearly every day at first to create a habit. I had a 1,000-day streak at one point before I got my new phone and had to reinstall the app. As of this writing, I am up to 500 days, so that makes 1500 consecutive days of gratitude, which is over four years, and boy, am I grateful!

🗝 TOC Key: Unlocking Gratitude
"Good, Better, Best"

Good (1-3 things you are grateful for daily)

Good requires the least effort on your part and can be as simple as a thought about how it feels when you pet an animal. You can quickly jot down the name of the pet and/or the type of pet. "Buddy, the dog," would work, or "petting cat." If you want to get even simpler, dog or cat works.

Better (2-3 things you are grateful for daily)

It's the same scenario, but better would be spending an extra 20-30 seconds thinking about what it is you love about petting an animal and making an effort to experience the joy more fully. Is it the fluffy fur, the warmth, the funny snoring sounds? Think about why you are so grateful for your pet. Imagine the sensations. Write down more details about your experience. (If you are not a pet lover, choose something else you love.)

Best (3+ daily)

If you have a pet nearby and can fully experience the moment, you can pet your animal and think more deeply about the reasons you are grateful. Create an image you can take wherever you go, like the one you created with the Sunshine Gaze TOC Key in Chapter 2. Your goal is to be able to recall this feeling in all of its richness at will. You also want to write down any nuances of your gratitude.

Now that you have the basic gist of how to use gratitude regularly, start thinking about a "go-to" list of your own that highlights things you are regularly grateful for. Do not be afraid to use the same one repeatedly. As I mentioned, I am often grateful for food, so some of my favorite menu items land on my gratitude list. Coffee is often on my list. The sky's the limit regarding what you can be thankful for on any given day. There are days when I rattle off 10 or more things that I appreciate in a matter of seconds.

Why Gratitude Works

While I am sure there is a more scientific explanation for why gratitude is so powerful, it boils down to directing your mind toward the positive to counteract any tendencies the brain has to lean negative. Most people find committing to a minimum of 21 days in a row helpful when establishing a new gratitude routine.

Once you get accustomed to looking for things in your life that make you feel glad, you may be surprised to find yourself celebrating "the little things" more often. Even the most stressed and anxious people I have had the opportunity to help have had tremendous success using gratitude to turn things around.

Gratitude in Action

Years ago, before I officially started focusing on the benefits of gratitude, I purchased a pair of running shoes, and the associate at the register accidentally left a big plastic anti-theft device on. Annoying, right? When I got home and realized what had happened, I quickly turned back around and headed out the door in a bit of a snit. On my way back to the shoe store, I spotted a passerby in a wheelchair who had no feet. Talk about a gratitude wake-up call. My mindset shifted instantly. As I get older, I am even more grateful for my ability to walk, as sometimes my feet hurt more than I would like them to. Walking is one of the joys in my life, and I do not take it for granted.

Expressing Gratitude Toward Others

We can also share how we feel when someone has done something we appreciate. Gratitude is for everyone, and giving thanks to others has a way of making us feel joyous, too. I get so much pleasure from offering kudos when I receive great customer service or when my honey does something on my honey-do list without being asked. I nearly fell over with gratitude, thanking the doctor who saved my eyesight. It is nice to be nice and let people know when they do a good job.

I have also gotten joy from donating to organizations or doing volunteer work I believe in. Even a small donation with a note letting others know I am grateful can impact my own mindset. When you eat a meal at a restaurant, for example, there are farmers, delivery drivers, managers, utensil manufacturers, servers, and many others who have played a role in your lunch. While you can't necessarily thank all of these people in person, you can acknowledge them in your mind. I learned this technique from the late Buddhist teacher, Thich Nhat Hanh.

Being Grateful When Things Are "Bad"

Whether you have been through a divorce, lost a child or parent, or been the victim of a violent crime, you are not likely to want to express gratitude immediately. Who would? While having a "bad" experience has its upsets, it also can teach us valuable lessons regarding things like who to marry, how to take care of our health, and what to do to avoid future danger. Being grateful even when someone has not performed perfectly is important as well. Think of the schoolteacher who only chastises students when the answers are wrong but fails to give positive feedback for work well done. Does that work out well?

A dog trainer who feeds a puppy treats for a job well done rather than punishing him when he falls short will get him to sit quickly and easily during a training session. In business, managers who are quick to point out what their employees are doing right and suggest corrections when staff fall short of expectations tend to have lower staff turnover rates. As a final example, a spouse who makes an effort to heap praise on their partner rather than criticism will foster an environment of mutual gratitude.

🔑 TOC Key: Express Gratitude for The Little Things

It's the little things (in life that bring us joy).

"It's the little things" is one of my favorite slogans. By starting small and creating a habit, you will gradually shift your mindset toward the wonderful little things in life. If your challenges feel insurmountable, and sometimes they will, gratitude is one of the easiest ways to get more joy in the moment without changing a single thing or using any of the other TOC Keys. Taking a short moment to celebrate even one positive thing a day will help you downplay the negative by default.

A gratitude habit won't make all of your worries go away, but fortunately, there are additional TOC Keys you can add to your optimism keychain. Gratitude is just one among many techniques that can get you started.

Why We Need More Gratitude

It was difficult to choose the quote at the beginning of this chapter, and because gratitude means so much to me, I wanted to share a few other quotes I really like before we go on to our next topic of mindfulness.

"There is a calmness to a life lived in gratitude, a quiet joy."
— Ralph H. Blum

"The more you linger in gratitude, the more you draw your new life to you."
"Gratitude is the ultimate state of receivership."
— Dr. Joe Dispenza

"Gratitude opens your eyes to the limitless potential of the universe."
— Stephen Richards

"Gratitude turns what we have into enough."
— Melody Beattie

"Acknowledging the good that you already have in your life is the foundation for all abundance."
— Eckhart Tolle

Next Up

You will learn a wide variety of methods for using mindfulness without the need for meditation in the following chapter.

Keeping your attention focused on the present is another way to live with greater optimism and joy when things don't go how you would like them to. We'll explore this together as we continue to add keys to our TOC keychain.

OPTIMISM DECODER

Chapter 3
Becoming Grateful For Nothing and Everything

- **Creating the habit of identifying things you can be grateful for every day is a powerful way to increase your optimism.**

- **There are little things in your life that you can appreciate with gratitude even when you are going through rough times.**

- **Giving praise to others in gratitude can be a powerful way to reap emotional benefits and boost your spirits.**

- **There are various ways to build gratitude into your life in order to make it a daily habit.**

- **Once you start focusing on things to be grateful for, your brain will naturally start noticing more of them.**

https://theoptimismcode.com

Chapter 4

Living Life in The Present Moment (Even When it Stinks)

"Breathing in, I calm my body. Breathing out,
I smile… I know this is a wonderful moment."

Thich Nhat Hanh

I remember when I first found out about the concept of mindfulness. I thought, *Why on earth would I want to be in the present moment when my present stinks like 3-day-old fish?* I tried to meditate but couldn't concentrate for more than about five seconds. I kept going into monkey mind mode. Like a tree-swinging primate high on bananas, I moved from past to future and back again as I traversed the jungle that was my overactive mind. No matter how hard I tried to stay focused, I kept getting sidetracked with random thoughts and felt formal meditation was next to impossible. If you have tried meditating when upset, you will relate to what I am saying here.

I later found out that mindfulness, which I will define more clearly in a moment, can be achieved without needing any meditation. What a relief! I have since learned various ways to bring my thoughts back to the present using traditional meditation techniques, but there are days when non-meditation mindfulness is easier. If I have nerve pain or lack resilience due to repeated stressors, non-meditation mindfulness, which I have abbreviated as NMM, can be easier.

Mindfulness Explained

So, what is mindfulness anyway, and why should we care? Mindfulness has a few definitions, but basically, it's an awareness of the present moment, ideally without judgment. When we are mindful, we focus on what is happening inside our mind and body while acknowledging external variables with as much neutrality as possible.

Training yourself to become mindful, whether by meditation or non-meditation methods, is a powerful step toward putting yourself in the driver's seat when managing emotions. It allows you to take control of the reins, so to speak, and steer yourself toward greater peace of mind in any given moment. Rather than living life as if you are on a runaway horse, you can learn how to bring attention back from the past and prevent worrisome, non-productive thoughts about your future from taking hold against your will.

Truth be told, you may want to focus on a situation from the past to make better decisions now or plan appropriately for the future. The trick is to be able to switch gears rather than allowing your primitive inner monkey mind to take charge. When you are on autopilot, it's easy to miss important signals that guide you to greater happiness.

Mindful Pam

I had a client, Pam, who had a habit of vilifying others whenever they didn't meet her expectations. By becoming mindful of her bodily sensations, she realized that every time she did this, she was triggering a stress response that made her feel ill.

Due to her upbringing, the pattern had become a reflex whenever people didn't act in a way that she deemed acceptable. She put them in the "bad" category as her brain grappled with the discrepancy between what she wanted to happen and what actually happened.

Now when her brain does this, she immediately notices how it makes her feel in the moment and has learned to shift her thoughts to a kinder stance. She recognizes that most of the time, letting others off the hook by recognizing we are all flawed is better for her own well-being. This allows Pam to make better, more rational decisions that are truly in her best interest and keeps her from agonizing over others' imperfections.

Paying Attention

By paying attention to your thoughts, feelings, and sensations as a mindful thinker, you will gain a greater appreciation of "the little things," as discussed in Chapter 3 on gratitude, and be in a position to maneuver life's twists and turns in a way that is more beneficial to you. The self-awareness that comes with mindfulness can be used to cope with chronic pain, improve physiological health, and relax more easily when confronted with stressors. Mindfulness has been studied extensively and has many other benefits that we won't get too deeply into, as I want to give you practical guidance and cut to the chase.

Mindfulness has allowed me to make powerful choices between acceptance and avoidance in real-time. Now that I am keenly aware of the present moment and can shift my attention from past to present to future, I have become much more tolerant of things I can't control. I can take decisive action now and plan better for the future. Mindfulness has also been instrumental in helping me to adopt better self-talk and refute distorted thinking, combating negativity that was weighing me down. I will be getting into the finer nuances of self-talk in Chapter 6.

🔑 TOC Key: Hot Shower Mindfulness

Have you ever taken a hot shower in the morning and realized your mind was racing forward to your to-do list rather than focusing on the task at hand?

The next time you shower (or bathe), notice how the water feels on your skin.

- Pay attention to how the soap and shampoo feel on your body.
- Watch the suds as they go down the drain.
- Make a note of the water temperature, the tile color, any thoughts and feelings you experience.
- When your mind wanders, bring your focus back to the moment and direct your attention to only what you are doing.
- If the water temperature is pleasing, you might even take a moment to express gratitude.

This is mindfulness!

When I take a bath with Epsom salt to ease aches and pains, I often catch myself sighing spontaneously. I have a particular appreciation for hot water after living in the West Indies in my late 20s with only rainwater collected from the gutters and no modern plumbing. When you think about it, it's pretty remarkable that heated water flows out a pipe into your home.

By paying attention mindfully, it's easier to drop my worries and focus on the joy of the moment, no matter what the past few hours have been like. Learning the art of shifting attention to the present moment instead of thinking about the "stinky" past or the worrisome future is so valuable. I see mindfulness as a superpower that needs to be developed. Once you master the various ways to get mindful in the moment, you can direct your thoughts and feelings in a split second.

Another Walking Story – Street Sweeper

I was walking in my neighborhood the other day. As I walked, rather than thinking about my work or grocery list, I was purposefully paying attention to my senses in a pseudo-meditative state. I noticed the smell of the crisp air, the beauty of the clouds in the sky, and the colorful plants in my neighbor's yard. It was bliss. As I passed the buttonwood tree, I reached out to feel its velvety soft leaves. I zeroed in on my breath, taking a big, deep inhale and holding it for an extra moment. Slowly, I released the air, and then it happened. Bam!

The street sweeper came toward me, lights flashing and scrubbers gyrating. I was definitely in the present moment when I had to make a quick decision or get mowed down by the machinery. Since I tend to be sensitive to noise, I instantly whipped out my handy earplugs. From my mindfulness practice, I have learned how to manage noise disruptions to maintain my sanity.

In theory, I could notice the street sweeper without judgment, but the fact of the matter is, I prefer peace and quiet while I am on my morning walks, so I avoided faulting myself for getting agitated. Instead, I used mindfulness to take swift action. I quickly turned down a side street to avoid the noxious vehicle, earplugs in place, and continued on my merry way, accepting the moment but taking steps to honor my needs. In a perfect world, mindfulness should be non-judgmental, but I can attest this is easier said than done. Please do your best not to judge yourself for judging yourself.

A Minor Nuisance

For some of you reading this, the street sweeper may seem trivial, and it is. Certainly, seeing a street sweeper is not a calamity by any stretch of the imagination. Nevertheless, being mindful to protect myself from an unpleasant experience that is easy enough to avoid is a matter of pragmatism. Instead of feeling like a victim of the big bad street sweeper, I get to be empowered and keep my nervous system from unnecessary overload. If I had forgotten to bring my earplugs and had to stay on the same street for whatever reason, I might have used an alternative coping strategy. Maybe some breathing exercises or helpful self-talk to remind me it's a minor nuisance that will be over shortly.

As you practice the various techniques that help bring you to a state of mindfulness, you will strengthen your ability to identify effective ways to maneuver the big and small irritations you will inevitably encounter. At times, the best strategy will be to accept what is, and at other times, you will lean on plan B, finding ways to mitigate a situation and taking care of yourself as best you can. When we are not mindful, the various options available for handling a given situation may not be apparent. This is one reason mindfulness is crucial to living life with maximum optimism.

Jennifer's Knees

Let me give you another quick example of why mindfulness is key to maintaining an optimistic attitude and taking care of your needs in real-time. My client, Jennifer, has chronic knee pain. When I met her, she spent a lot of time wallowing in self-pity and had what I consider a "woe is me" mindset. "My knees hurt, and I am sick of having this pain. Life stinks, and I will never be able to walk normally again," she would say.

I recognized Jennifer's habit of catastrophizing and guided her to mindfully notice times throughout the day when her pain was stronger and when the pain was more tolerable. This helped Jennifer realize her knees didn't "always" hurt severely. The pain only flared sometimes, and at other times, when she was distracted or rested for a while, she hardly noticed the discomfort.

As I worked with Jennifer, I coached her to develop a new script surrounding her situation and use mindfulness strategies to uncover counterproductive thoughts and behaviors that might be making the pain worse. I also aided her in taking practical steps by choosing natural remedies and different footwear.

This combined effort significantly reduced Jennifer's pain and improved her attitude about her discomfort. While Jennifer still has knee pain from time to time, by focusing on her thoughts, feelings, and behaviors using mindfulness, Jennifer has created a plan that allows her to maintain a more positive attitude.

Relax Your Mind With Mindfulness

Mindfulness can also be used effectively as a relaxation strategy to take a break from the monkey chatter of the mind. When I spend even a few minutes per day using my own mindfulness TOC Keys, it gives me a chance to relax. Don't worry if it feels nearly impossible for you to relax. You'll get the hang of it as we progress, even if your monkey mind sometimes feels like an 800-pound gorilla.

Breathing 101

One of my favorite ways to rest my weary brain and bring my body back to a serene state of relaxation is through breath exercises. Everyone has to breathe, right? So why not breathe in a way that leads to greater well-being? When we are worked up, our breath becomes shallow, and we don't even realize it until it's too late. When we take the time to breathe properly, we lower our stress hormones and quiet the storm in our minds.

If I could pick only one non-meditation mindfulness habit for anxiety reduction, it would be breathing for relaxation. How is your breath right now as you read this? Is it deep or shallow? Pay attention in this moment without making any changes just yet.

Before we go any further, I want to mention that if you have any cardio-pulmonary or cerebral health issues like epilepsy, please be extra cautious with any breathing technique you adopt. This book is for educational purposes only, and I don't want anyone to pass out. Even if you are in tip-top health, I recommend sitting down as you explore the various breathing techniques we will look at, as deep breathing can significantly lower blood pressure. For some, this is a good thing, but I want you to avoid hurting yourself, so be careful.

TOC Keys: Breathing Exercises

🔑 Slow and Long

My personal favorite and the easiest type of breathing is the slow and long method. Ideally, this should be a diaphragmatic breath from your belly, in through your nose, and out through your mouth slowly, but don't let perfection get in your way. If you are unfamiliar with "diaphragmatic breathing," there are multiple videos online to guide you.

Basically, all you need to do is exhale any excess air you are holding in your lungs and breathe in through your nose until your lungs are full. Next, hold your breath for as long as is comfortable. Then, slowly, and I mean slowly, breathe out. The slower the better. You should feel relaxed by the time you are done. That's it. Pretty simple, right? If you still feel like you need another one in times of stress, repeat the process for several rounds.

Feel free to count as you go or use a short mantra like, "peace, calm, joy," for example, as you breathe in and out. This will help you stay in a mindful state rather than letting your thoughts wander. As long as you are comfortable, you can do this breathing technique as many times as you like until you notice a quieting of the mind and your body loosening up. If you have recently become upset by a stressful event, it may take a little longer to get into a calm state, so keep at it until you notice a significant improvement in how you feel.

🔑 Box Breathing

One popular method of breathing you may want to try is known as box breathing. It's more structured than the "slow and long" method. All you have to do, ideally using diaphragmatic breath—in through the nose and out through the mouth—is to inhale, hold to the count of four, exhale to four, and hold again. Go slowly for best results. This technique can be done any time you take a work break or notice your breath has been shallow. Until you feel confident you can do so while walking or driving, this should be done only while seated for starters until you know how it affects you. Dizziness is no fun.

Inhale, 2, 3, 4

Hold, 2, 3, 4

Exhale, 2, 3, 4

Pause, 2, 3, 4

🔑 Triangle Breathing

A shorter version of box breathing is triangle breathing. It's good for those who are a bit impatient and is considered a great choice if you are public speaking with anxiety beforehand. Breathe in for three seconds, hold for three seconds, and release for three seconds. Again, you can either count the numbers -2-3 or use a mantra like "safe, calm, secure." Alternately, you can inhale to the count of three, saying "safe" in your head. Hold the word "calm" and then exhale as you say "secure " to yourself.

This breathing exercise does not have a pause like box breathing does, so you want to go straight back into the inhale for another triangle round. Decide what works best for you. The most important thing to remember is that you can almost always use one form of breathing or another as you go about your day to keep stress and anxiety from escalating. Once you get into the habit, you will start using this key naturally.

🔑 Meditative Breathing

At the beginning of this chapter, I quoted Thich Nhat Hanh, a Buddhist monk who spent many years teaching mindfulness before passing in 2022 at the age of 95. This modified method can be used during formal meditation or while fully awake and alert.

Breathing in, *I calm my body*.

Breathing out, I smile.

After you breathe out, take a brief moment and smile before continuing. This technique is good if you are in public, as nobody will really notice other than seeing you start smiling. It is also great for use during business meetings.

🔑 Listen and Do Nothing

To get back to breathing without changing anything, simply notice your breath and the rise of your chest cavity. Pay attention to your breath without intentionally modifying the flow. You may have an occasional deeper breath as you focus. If you lose track of your breathing, come back to it. Notice how the air feels entering your nostrils and exiting your body through your nose or mouth. Follow it for as long as possible and correct it whenever your mind wanders.

Bottom Line on Breathing

There are so many ways to breathe for mood-boosting and stress reduction. Experiment, and if you like, run a search to identify potential online resources as you incorporate breathing exercises into your new, more optimistic life.

Optimism and Mindfulness

As I began practicing mindfulness with formal meditation and non-meditation methods, I realized that mindfulness is especially important when life throws us "stinky" situations. It's difficult to remain optimistic when you aren't mindful of your thoughts, feelings, and sensations as they occur. By paying attention, you enable yourself to step in on your own behalf to make shifts in your attitude, behaviors, and self-talk.

In addition to breathing techniques, Chapter 5 will explore a slew of brain hacks and mind-body practices that do not require formal meditation. Some of them may seem a little weird or woo-woo at first, but don't be afraid to give them a try; they can do wonders for reducing stress and anxiety.

An Aside—End of Chapter Gratitude Exercise

Thich Nhat Hanh also shared a great gratitude exercise you can try. The next time you have a meal or get a package in the mail, take a few seconds to think about every person in the supply chain who may have contributed. If you are eating a salad, for example, imagine the person who sold the vegetable seeds to the farmer. Think about the people who watered the fields and harvested the crops. Envision the factory worker packing the lettuce for transport. Give kudos to the unknown truck driver who traveled across the country with your produce. Imagine the supermarket employees who stocked shelves, checked you out at the cash register or bagged your veggies.

There is so much to be grateful for in that one little salad. Now breathe and smile!

OPTIMISM DECODER

Chapter 4
Living Life in The Present Moment
(Even When it Stinks)

- Mindfulness allows you to focus on the present moment instead of dwelling on the past or future.

- When we are mindful, we are able to identify pragmatic solutions to improve our well-being in the moment.

- Being mindful can be accomplished through non-meditation methods in addition to traditional meditation practices.

- There are breathing techniques that can be used as part of a mindfulness plan to reduce stress and anxiety.

- No matter what is going on in your life, mindfulness can bring you into the present moment to improve optimism quickly.

https://theoptimismcode.com

Chapter 5

Hacking Your Untamed Brain Without Meditation (Really!)

"Enjoy the little things, for one day you may look back and realize they were the big things."

Robert Brault

Enjoying the little things involves paying attention in the moment to what you are experiencing. We covered breathing in the last chapter, but breathing is just one example of a mindfulness exercise you can do. The good news is that there are many other ways to develop mindfulness throughout your day without formal meditation practice.

While the mind-body hacks in this chapter are not likely to turn you into an overjoyed optimist overnight, they play an important role as you fill your life with more joy. By boosting endorphin levels and prompting you to direct attention toward the present, these methods are stepping-stones toward exponentially elevating your mood.

During the process of writing this book, there were times when I had tremendous feelings of overwhelm. As a solo-preneur on a mission to help one million people live with greater optimism, getting my books, courses, and coaching tools out into the world felt daunting at times. Websites, funnels, podcasts, it was all mind-boggling. As my head spun with thoughts of how to roll out The Optimism Code, I used the following mindfulness exercise to bring myself back to the here and now.

When you feel overwhelmed by work, current events, or a never-ending list of household chores, you can use this same strategy to transform worrisome thoughts in minutes.

🔑 TOC Key: What's Happening Now?

If your to-do list feels like it's too much and you are starting to spiral into a pessimistic mindset, I recommend trying this simple mindfulness exercise as soon as you catch yourself ruminating. It's very simple: Become awake and aware of exactly what you are doing at the moment.

Here is a simplistic example to give you an idea of how easy it is to change your thoughts.

TRIGGER: Feeling overwhelmed by the magnitude of the tasks that need to be accomplished during your work week.

TOC STRATEGY: Shift focus toward only what is going on in the present moment.

Here's an example of how I went through my own step-by-step process using the "What's Happening Now?" technique to move away from stressful, counterproductive thoughts. I tuned into my senses to shift gears and stop fueling my anxiety about the busy day ahead. By focusing on what I was seeing, touching, tasting, hearing, and smelling, I was able to take charge of my runaway thoughts quickly.

Getting Present: As soon as I caught my monkey mind ruminating, I asked myself what was happening now. I happened to be pouring myself a glass of ice water. Here is what I said to regain my focus using all of my senses.

1. I'm getting ice from the freezer and putting it into the cup I just got from the cupboard. (Sight)

2. The ice feels cool to the touch as my hands place it in the cup. (Touch)

3. The water is clear, and I hear it as I pour it out of the gallon jug over the ice cubes. (Sight / Sound)

4. I take a nice big sip and focus on how grateful I am to have fresh, clean water. (Taste)

By the time I finished pouring my "mindful" glass of water, I was no longer racking my brain about all the things that needed to get done. Instead, I interrupted the pattern and put all of those feelings of overwhelm on the back burner where they belonged, freeing myself to accomplish the day's tasks in manageable bits and pieces.

A secondary method for the "What's Happening Now?" exercise is to name things in your environment for 30 seconds or so. When you see, hear, touch, taste, or smell items in your surroundings, briefly describe them with just one or two adjectives and a noun to bring you back to the moment. In the example above, I could have thought, *White icemaker, sickle-shaped ice, green plastic cup, cool hands, clear, fresh water, plastic jug, quenched thirst, silver freezer door, etc.*

Tim's Traffic Woes

I remember one client, we'll call him Tim, who frequently became anxious when driving, which was required for his sales job. He loathed slow-moving traffic, which had become an automatic trigger for thoughts about his future with the company. Tim had developed a habit of letting stop-and-go traffic jams snowball into worries about his long-term career. I taught Tim to use this technique whenever he started to drift into worry about his ability to manage a "road warrior" job that required heavy travel.

Tim watched and named what was happening right in front of him instead of fretting over potential future events. "Red light, yellow line, green tree, silver barricade, blue sports car, white arrow, beige steering wheel, jazz music, air conditioning." Every time he used this simple trick, he would laugh about how much energy he had spent worrying about slow-moving traffic that he had absolutely no control over. The truth was that despite these weekly road trips, which were not his favorite thing to do, Tim loved his job as a whole. By using this technique whenever he came to a slowdown while driving, he brought himself back to the moment and broke the pattern of rumination he had developed.

If Tim truly felt that driving was something he 100% did not want to do in the future, this exercise would still have been helpful. It would have allowed Tim to become more of an observer and make a conscious decision about his future with a clear head. He might have noticed the tightness in his jaw and gut, deciding that pursuing a different career path with no travel would be worth it.

Music Calms the Savage Beast

If Tim had wanted to, he could have listened to music or a podcast to distract himself. Singing or humming to one of his favorite tunes out loud could have boosted his spirits and helped him refocus his attention toward something positive. I personally love to listen to tunes that remind me of happy moments in my life. You know, the kind of song where you know all the words by heart and get excited when it comes on the radio. There are some good studies on the benefits of music. I have been caught more than once at a red light having a blast while driving alone. Humming can also be an effective stress reliever. When I take a hot bath, I sometimes hum underwater for a few seconds and find it extremely soothing.

Another way to get your head back into the moment with sounds is by listening to singing bowls. They are not for everyone, but many people find the sound they make incredibly relaxing. Whether doing a formal meditation or just looking for calming background noise, listening to binaural beats is incredibly soothing. Binaural beats occur in music with differing tones that go from one ear to the other. They are best listened to with headphones and have positive pain management, sleep, and relaxation benefits. You can keep them in the background while working or even listen with earbuds when running errands.

Another way to add positive sound to your life is with hang or tongue drum music. This type of music can be particularly helpful when you have aches and pains. While there is limited research on the topic, these "complex drumming" sounds have been shown to reduce physical discomfort. As someone who suffers from chronic, widespread pain, I can attest to the benefits of complex drumming in addition to binaural beats.

Zeroing in on nuanced drumbeats helps your brain shift focus and somehow "forget" the pain. You can easily find this type of music online. If you would like a few suggestions, please visit the Optimism Code website listed in the resources section at the end of the book.

Dance

While I am not the best dancer, I am a big fan of doing modified Zumba at home and, in particular, enjoy Soca-style Caribbean music. Moving your body can impact your mood quickly, and dancing is one of those activities that allow you to express yourself freely. The next time you listen to one of your favorite songs and have the opportunity, take a minute to get up and dance. When I'm in a bad mood, amazingly, less than one minute of calypso can almost always lift my spirits. Even an armchair dance can be beneficial if you are at your office desk or don't have full mobility. Most forms of physical activity can release mood-boosting endorphins into the bloodstream.

Mind-Body Somatic Exercises

Mind-body exercises are designed to move you from anxious to relaxed in a matter of seconds and are a great alternative to formal meditation. Experiment to see which methods you like best so you can add a few of your favorites to your optimism keychain.

🔑 TOC Key: NMM Scan

No, the NMM Scan is not some new sort of medical test. NMM is an acronym that stands for "Non-Meditation Mindfulness." These quick and easy practices can be done with eyes wide open, and some can even be done while driving.

There are three parts to the NMM Scan.

1. Assess your body for aches, pains, discomforts, tension, etc. Going from the top down, how is your head? Is your jaw clenched? What does your stomach feel like? Do you notice any tension in your torso or limbs? How are your feet doing?

2. Next, do the scan a second time. This time, instead of focusing on what is wrong in the moment, go from top to bottom listing any body part that feels at ease, relaxed, or neutral. I almost never have pain or tension in my calves, for example. The goal is to be mindful of those areas of your body that don't hurt and can easily go unnoticed.

3. The last step of the NMM Scan is to return to each tense or uncomfortable body part and focus on relaxing your muscles area by area. If your jaw is tight, loosen it up by gently dropping the lower half so your tongue hangs comfortably. You can even move your jaw around if you like. A quick external massage of the area where the jaw hinges can also be helpful.

While many of you may be familiar with body scans, this method is a quick way to bring you back to the present and create awareness so you can eliminate tightness in your body, signaling your brain that it's okay to relax. A NMM Scan is a great way to re-center yourself during a busy workday or traveling. I taught Tim, the client I mentioned earlier in this chapter, to use the NMM Scan while en route to his next sales call as an additional strategy to reduce his anxiety.

🔑 TOC Key: Quick-Fix Relaxation Response

Roughly half a century ago, Dr. Herbert Benson, a Harvard cardiologist, developed a method known as the Relaxation Response to counteract the negative effects of stress and anxiety. This Quick-Fix TOC Key is an adaptation of his technique designed specifically for busy, on-the-go people.

When I do this exercise, I like to scrunch my facial muscles as tight as I can and make a fist with both hands. You can add a shoulder shrug, too, if you like. Once you have tightened your face, hands, and neck muscles, clench for about 10 seconds or until it begins to feel noticeably uncomfortable.

This exercise is good to do in the restroom if you're somewhere where breathing exercises might not be the best idea, if you catch my drift. Even if you are sitting at a cubicle desk, this can be a quick strategy to restore peace of mind.

The Quick-Fix relaxation response creates a brief interval of mindfulness and a pleasant relaxation boost when you don't have much time. When you are not in a restroom, combining this with deep breathing and slow exhales can be a double treat to bring you into a better state of mind after a stressful event.

🔑 TOC Keys: The Eyes Have It

These eye movements are super helpful when you have a very active monkey mind. When I do this exercise, I can literally feel the shift. My monkey mind quiets down as thoughts from the back of my brain settle, and the executive function in my forehead comes online. I am able to think more clearly instantly. There are two ways to do this exercise.

1. 🔑 **Eye Rolling**: While sitting or standing, roll your eyes up as if trying to look at the center point at the top of your head. Hold your eyes in this position for as long as you can, at least 10-20 seconds. Once finished, you can relax your eyes and look straight ahead as you normally would.

    You can either repeat this a few times or try an alternate method—position your eyes at the top left corner of your field of vision for about 10-15 seconds, then switch to the opposite top right corner, looking up and to the right for as long as you can. Feel free to combine this with the breathing routine of your choice and a quick smile for an extra boost of optimism.

2. 🔑 **Eye Palming:** Another way to release tension around your eyes is to gently place the base of your palms around your eye sockets with your fingers pointed upwards, cradling your head. Your thumbs should be pointed outward near your temples and can be used for a brief massage. I find this very calming when I have been through a particularly stressful event. If you want to, you can add a rocking motion to relax even more if your anxiety levels have spiked.

3. 🔑 **Staring:** Your eyes can also be used effectively to calm you by staring at a fireplace or a candle. Staring at any point on a wall can put you into a state of mindfulness and relax you. You can combine counting down from five to one and back again while breathing methodically.

    When I was a little girl, and my father was on his way home from work in the days before cell phones, my mother and I would wait out on the porch for him, and she would call it contemplating. We would sit, doing nothing but staring at the lawn and nearby shrubs. Whether you focus on a candle or a point on the wall, staring meditation, also referred to as Trataka, can be a powerful and effective way to relax your mind.

All you need to do is maintain your focus on one point. In addition to improving concentration, it can help you to feel more peaceful. One of my favorite ways of practicing Trataka is to stare at a fireplace during winter and watch the flames dance. I find it incredibly soothing.

🔑 TOC Keys: Self-Care-ess Strategies

There are several techniques you can use to boost your endorphins on an ongoing basis that are rooted in science. Our sense of touch is a great connection to well-being that often goes untapped when stressed.

1. 🔑 Easy Hand Care-ess

Even if people surround you, you can easily take the fingers of one hand and run them over the top of your other hand, starting from your wrist and ending between your fingers. This exercise can also be done in the opposite direction by placing your fingers from one hand over your fingers on the other hand and moving toward your wrist. However, this may be more obvious if you are in a business meeting, so I recommend you put your hands on your lap for privacy. This simple act will boost oxytocin, the love hormone, which has been shown to help those who suffer from depression.

2. 🔑 **Wrist and Arm Care-essing**

I use this version of Care-essing quite a bit while lying on the couch or even when meditating and having difficulty getting into a deeper meditative state. In this version, you take one hand and start at your inner wrist, working your way up to just above your inner elbow, also known as your elbow pit. Keep your fingers spread and use a light touch for maximum benefit. Feel free to explore the region to identify the areas that feel best to you. You can even go higher up on the softer underside of your arm if you like.

3. 🔑 **Facial Care-essing**

The face also has many nerve endings that respond well to touch, particularly at the edge of the neck. You can run the spread fingers of your right hand along your left jawline across your face and even allow your fingers to caress your lips.

Making a habit of doing any of these exercises is a good way to increase your feel-good chemicals with minimal effort. Rather than going for food or alcohol to calm your nerves, try this instead the next time you get worked up. Feel free to combine any of these Self-Care-ess strategies with neck massage as well as deep breathing if desired.

There are a variety of other methods that can be used effectively to quell uneasy feelings that crop up when you are faced with stress, whether you have a time-sensitive business deadline, haven't slept well, or are irritated by a bad customer service experience (We have all been there!) Experimenting to see what works for you is what it's all about. No one technique will be effective for everyone, so I want to provide you with a few additional options as you begin your journey to greater optimism.

🔑 EFT: Tapping

Tapping, also known as Emotional Freedom Technique (EFT), is a method you may or may not already be familiar with. It doesn't resonate with everyone, but for those who enjoy it, tapping can be quite effective. Multiple new studies regularly point to its benefits. I had an app that was quite good, and I know several people who use tapping regularly. Check out our resources section for more info if you want to learn more.

🔑 Hobbies

Hobbies like puzzles, knitting, coloring (Mandalas are good), building ship models, painting, etc. can also be very therapeutic. Any hobby that keeps your mind focused on the activity at hand is helpful for boosting your mood and improving brain health, but don't sniff the glue if you decide to assemble a replica of a boat. I personally love a good jigsaw puzzle, but I now use a phone app to keep my living room from becoming a mess. It's not quite the same, but it does the trick.

The other added benefit of a hobby is that hobbies allow us to have a sense of mastery. Be sure to choose wisely, though, to set yourself up for success rather than failure. Doing the NY Times crossword puzzle, which is a bit challenging, may lead to frustration. Better to start out with something you will be successful at and work your way up to greater levels of difficulty over time.

68

🔑 Journaling

Another common non-meditation mindfulness (NMM) strategy that many benefit from is journaling. However, be sure not to let your journal become a place where all you do is gripe about the negative. While it's good to get your feelings out on paper, don't forget you can also use your journal to document the positive. Your journal can be used to list things you are grateful for and even to develop new positive self-talk statements. I sometimes journal to reverse negative what-iffing as it helps to write down the positive outcomes I am hoping for to combat worry.

🔑 Essential Oils

While I don't personally use essential oils often, I have clients who report achieving great benefits from soothing scents. Whether you go with lavender, citrus, or frankincense, essential oils can potentially aid you with relaxation. One woman told me she put a couple of drops in her shower, and the experience was quite relaxing. She tried peppermint and shared that it made her eyes water, so proceed cautiously. Look for quality brands with a solid reputation if you add essential oils as one of the keys on your optimism keychain.

🔑 Viewing Images

When I go for my morning walks, I get the opportunity to get out in the fresh air and experience nature. I enjoy looking online at images of flowers, animals, and smiling faces when I can't get out, whether due to illness or inclement weather. (My puzzle app has some great nature photos.) Even 1-3 minutes of viewing videos of happy pets or people can help. As you watch the videos, try adding a smile of your own for an extra boost of joy.

🔑 Hot and Cold Therapy

The use of both heat and ice can be beneficial for mood boosting. I have tried to take a cold shower but can't make myself do it regularly. Many people report amazing benefits from cold plunges. I do find taking an ice cube and holding it in my hand, or swimming in cold water, does seem to have the positive effect of lifting my spirits. I recommend experimenting with cold to see what feels right to you. I prefer heat and enjoy using a heating pad during the winter months when I am doing traditional meditation. I find it very soothing. The bottom line when it comes to hot or cold therapy is to trust your instincts.

🔑 Yoga and Stretching

I wish I could get more into yoga. My monkey mind has always struggled with formal yoga, and now that I have more aches and pains, I honestly find it a challenge. Luckily, there are many yoga options for those with good flexibility who enjoy it. If yoga is not your thing, you can still benefit from simple stretching. Whether you do it yourself, choose an online class, or go with a personal instructor, several forms of yoga are as therapeutic as formal meditation when it comes to improving mindfulness.

🔑 Compassion Meditation

Okay, so technically, this practice has the word meditation in it, but I always do this technique while fully alert. Kristin Neff is well known for developing this method. It includes a series of mantras that begin with wishing yourself well and then wishing wellness upon your loved ones, strangers, and even those you are angry with. I find it very helpful for creating a space of forgiveness for both myself and others. I say, "May I be happy, may I be well, may I be comfortable, and at peace." You can add words like safe, healthy, etc. to customize your compassion meditation.

🔑 Reiki

While I consider Reiki a little woo-woo, when I do Self-care-ess techniques, I will sometimes add my own adaptation to ease jaw tightness. I move my hand about an inch from my face so I can feel the heat coming off of my hand onto my face. I then make a circular motion without actually touching my face. Don't ask me how this works, but I find it relaxing. I have not had the opportunity to go to a Reiki practitioner, but I find this fascinating. I suspect there are electromagnetic fields we can't see when it comes to the benefits of Reiki.

The Bottom Line

I'm sure I've left a few other mind-body strategies off of this list, but this should give you lots of good ideas to improve your mindset using your own physiology. By choosing even a few of these methods regularly, your body chemistry will shift toward joy and positivity.

In the next chapter, I will focus on ways you can tame your mind further by developing a new system of self-talk I have dubbed "TOC Talk." TOC Talk blends slogans, popular clichés, affirmations, and reframing techniques to help you achieve maximum optimism.

OPTIMISM DECODER

Chapter 5
Hacking Your Untamed Brain Without Meditation (Really!)

- In addition to breathing techniques, there are many mind-body hacks that can increase your mindfulness.

- Specific methods for zeroing in on the present moment can be implemented to help you de-stress without formal meditation.

- Somatic exercises including eye movements, self-care-essing, and music/dance boost en-dorphins to reduce anxiety.

- Other strategies like journaling, hobbies, and the use of essential oils can improve mindfulness as well.

- Combining non-meditation mindfulness (NMM) with gratitude habits and breathing exercises may boost positivity rapidly.

https://theoptimismcode.com

Chapter 6

Creating Your Own TOC Talk: The Language of Optimism

"Although the world is full of suffering, it is also full of the overcoming of it."

Helen Keller

What we say to ourselves in times of stress is often a reflection of what has been said to us as children. Both positive and negative messaging tends to be passed on from one generation to the next. By developing a strategy that combines slogans with standard clichés, we can literally reprogram our brain to lean more toward the positive and counteract negative thinking that doesn't serve us well.

TOC Talk, The Optimism Code's unique version of positive self-talk, has been designed to chip away at hard-wired thought patterns that can undermine us. Bringing attention through mindfulness to what you are saying to yourself in the present moment is only half of the equation. The other half is transforming those thoughts intentionally to boost your mood despite the unanticipated shake-ups that often spiral into negativity.

Managing Emotions with TOC Talk

Let's go through some of the unique slogans I have developed over the years that will help you manage your emotions in a more realistic and productive way. I also explain how you can use them along with clichés by following a simple three-question method designed to help you work through your feelings. You may want to highlight or check off some of the ones that resonate with you and add them to your optimism keychain later.

The phrases in brackets don't need to be included when you use them. They are added for deeper understanding. Once you know the meaning behind each slogan, you can truncate the sentence. One of the biggest challenges I have faced with most traditional cognitive behavioral therapy (CBT) strategies is that it's next to impossible to refute distorted thinking in the moment when I'm upset.

It's much easier to memorize shorter phrases that can be applied to multiple situations. This way, you can recall them quickly and easily whenever needed. That said, if the longer versions of a slogan help you more, by all means, use them. Your goal is to be able to fire off your TOC Talk automatically to counteract the well-grooved negative language patterns etched in your mind over many years.

It's worth mentioning that you will continue to have negative thoughts, particularly in the beginning. This is normal and to be expected, given the number of years your brain has been practicing repeating negative self-talk.

Below are a few examples of things people say to themselves. Can you spot one similar to what you tend to say to yourself when upset?

- I can't handle this situation.
- I'm not good enough. I never do anything right.

- I'm an idiot (or he/she is an idiot).

- What's wrong with me/them?

These are just a few examples of the milder things people say to themselves that can easily undermine joy. Once you memorize your favorite TOC Talk slogans, you will become a pro at overlaying them to counteract those original problematic thoughts you've grown accustomed to. I will explain more about how this works as we proceed, but for now, I want to go over each slogan individually, so you understand the meaning.

🔑 TOC Key: TOC Talk Slogans

Anyone in my shoes might feel the same way.

At times, it can feel pretty lonely when we're upset about a situation. If you've ever had someone tell you, "You shouldn't be upset," when you *are* upset, you know what I am talking about. You are not the only person who's felt this way. It's difficult for people to have empathy when something that bothers you doesn't bother them but mark my word; we all have something that pushes our buttons— every single one of us.

Realizing that you are not the only person who might feel upset in the same circumstances is powerful. It allows you to let yourself off the hook for your feelings. There is nothing wrong with you. Your feelings are what they are, so there is no need to reprimand yourself or tell yourself you shouldn't feel a certain way. While you may want to shift your mindset to feel differently, permitting yourself to feel as you do in the moment goes a long way toward preventing the kind of self-recrimination that often leads to the blues.

I recall one career coaching client of mine who had sent out 100 resumés and only received two job interviews. It would be unusual if she didn't feel a little upset about this. Of course, she was discouraged. Who wouldn't be? Telling herself that "anyone in her shoes might feel the same," kept her from spiraling down and allowed her to continue her job search. While we did take a realistic look at what she could do differently going forward to get better results, recognizing that she was having a normal reaction to her situation was helpful.

Being imperfect is okay. (Nobody else is perfect either.)

Holding onto the idea of perfection can be a real stumbling block for many people. It's so much easier to be imperfect. Lowering the bar doesn't mean we don't strive to be our personal best, but trying to attain perfection can be exhausting. What is perfection anyway? As I mentioned previously, I define myself as quirky and acknowledge that I have many imperfections. Still, I have learned over time to be proud of my strengths while downplaying my shortcomings. As Patricia Noll, author of the book *Good With Me,* says, "We are perfect in our imperfection and thereby human."

You will feel much better about yourself when you let yourself off the hook. This TOC Talk slogan can be helpful when dealing with others as well. Recognizing that friends, family, and coworkers are bound to fall short of your expectations is powerful. It prevents disappointment and resentment from taking hold. This doesn't mean you don't maintain standards for how people treat you. You want to set appropriate boundaries. It means that you realize that even people who love you and truly care can be imperfect, too, at times. We all have limitations. Most of the time, when people don't perform at the level we were hoping for, they don't do it on purpose. Taking a more realistic view of the human condition helps us prevent disappointment when we, or those around us, fall short.

There is nothing wrong with me (that isn't wrong with everyone else).

Believing that you are the only person who has challenges in life is erroneous, yet many people are extra hard on themselves. The fact is that while you may have one issue, your neighbor or co-worker may have another, different issue. We are all different, yet we are all the same. While this slogan is similar to the one about imperfection, it is more nuanced in stopping thoughts that you are somehow defective. You are not. You may have some aspect of your behavior you want to improve, but this does not make you a broken human being.

Change my focus (and my feelings will follow).

We have touched upon the importance of shifting your focus more than once, as this is an important skill for getting back to a place of optimism. Having a go-to mantra to remind you to take action is helpful. While valid, your feelings are often the result of what you are focusing on. Once you shift your focus, your feelings are also bound to shift.

My client Jane would often obsess about how her chronic fatigue was debilitating. While nobody wants to be exhausted all of the time, Jane did not have a medical answer to her illness. I asked her to do an exercise to identify what she was saying to herself. It turns out that Jane was saying things like, "I can't function," "I can never get anything done," "I have no energy," "I am useless," and more. I taught Jane to change her focus every time she caught herself trash-talking about her chronic fatigue. She came up with several things she could do even when she felt too tired to refocus her attention on the positive. This new change in mindset helped Jane to ignore her illness more, and as a result, she paradoxically began to feel less fatigued.

Do things in bits and pieces (so I don't get overwhelmed).

When I have a lot of incomplete to-dos, I sometimes notice my throat and stomach muscles getting tighter. I view this as my body's early warning signals, telling me it's time to slow it down and take things in bits and pieces. When you feel like you have more on your plate than you can manage, using this phrase can be extremely helpful. You can rapidly reduce anxious thoughts and feelings by reminding yourself to take a realistic look at your goals and identify items that can be broken down into smaller steps.

For example, imagine if I had tried to write this entire book without breaking it down into manageable sections. I can guarantee it would never have been written. Whether you tend to freeze like a deer caught in headlights or try to knock out everything on your to-do list at once, succumbing to burnout, using this "bits and pieces" slogan will help get you back on track.

Moods vary like the tide—we all have highs and lows.

This is a very important slogan when you feel sad or angry. It's easy to feel as though how you feel now will last forever. You may have situations in your life that are tumultuous with no clear resolution in sight. Situational upset, combined with self-blame, is a surefire way to land in "bad-mood-ville." It happens to the best of us. The important thing to know is that your mood is not forever. How you feel is temporary, and your spirits will lift again.

Similarly, if you are in a super elated state of mind, it's good to recognize that life is not one big party, and you may not have that level of zealousness tomorrow. A good example of this is what I refer to as the "vacation phenomenon." A large part of the excitement of a vacation is planning and looking forward to it. You may or may not have a smooth and pleasant experience on your journey; it's even possible that your trip could fall short of expectations. It's not uncommon to feel a little bummed out when the excursion is over. Your mood will likely lift again as soon as you plan a new vacation. Moods vary like the tide.

We can't always feel joyous every moment. Reminding ourselves that dark clouds will pass is very helpful. That said, accepting that you don't feel 100% overjoyed every moment of every day is important if you tend to be a black-and-white thinker, particularly when you are going through a rough situation.

It's not worth losing my peace of mind (or making myself sick).

There are times when negative thoughts can really spiral, particularly if something very upsetting occurs, like a fight with a good friend, a job layoff, or a teenager testing your patience. Whatever the cause, no matter what is going on, if you notice yourself spiraling in a way that's interfering with your day, this slogan will pull you back into the moment and remind you that well-being is your priority.

The day-to-day events of our lives are often insignificant years later. I call them the "problems du jour" because I know that no matter what occurs today, I may not even remember the troublesome situation a month or year from now. Why get myself in a dither? Stepping back to remember that this seemingly horrible happening will someday become a memory of the past is valuable. I find this a particularly helpful slogan for those going through a breakup or divorce.

Think back to your first love. How do you feel about the situation now that time has passed? My guess is that the sting of the event is much less intense. Your priority should always be to boost your levels of joy as quickly as possible. Sometimes you may need to lick your wounds and wallow in the "abyss of sorrow" for a little while but remember this slogan the next time you let your "problem du jour" get the best of you. I used this slogan just yesterday when I found myself having a pity party about my neck pain.

My beliefs are not necessarily true. (Not everyone sees the world in the same way.)

Some of the biggest misunderstandings at work, home, and out in the world stem from our belief systems. For example, I have a belief that people should say thank you if a door is held open for them. I also believe that people should use their directional signals when driving if they are turning. Not everyone does these things. Some people may believe it's unnecessary, or they may be preoccupied. Who knows? The bottom line is that their perception or their beliefs surrounding holding a door open or using a directional signal when driving may differ from mine.

I want to share a specific example to illustrate my point. When I first started dating my honey, he used to open the car door for me. Sounds great, right? I was very independent at the time and viewed this as somewhat patronizing for some bizarre reason, so I didn't like it very much. Fast forward to today, I absolutely adore it when he opens my car door. My beliefs shifted over time as my interpretation of his actions changed. I now see his car-door-opening as a sign of love and respect.

While this is a trivial example, it can be used to teach the value of recognizing that we all have different belief systems, and that one person is not necessarily right while another person is wrong. Beliefs are malleable and nuanced. Recognizing this can save you from unnecessary resentment based on high standards that may not be met by others. It can also help you to consider other viewpoints so you can transform your limiting beliefs and cognitive distortions with greater ease.

We can't always be on the same wavelength (as one another).

Even when our beliefs are similar, it's easy to misinterpret things that people say and do. We tend to see things through our own lens. We are all unique and our perceptions vary. Those of us who have worked in the corporate world know what it can be like when one department doesn't understand the motivations of another team. The result of frequent miscommunications can easily create challenges if project managers don't get everyone onto the same page.

Recognizing this can help us to feel less frustrated when interacting with others. As I write this, my neighbor is putting in a nice new kitchen. He has no idea that I am busy writing a book and find it distracting. His goal is to get his kitchen done. My goal is to get this book written per my deadline. We have competing needs and are not on the same wavelength.

All I can do is sequester myself in another room that is further away from our common wall. Such is condo life. Clearly, we are not on the same page at the moment, but it would be unrealistic of me to ask him to send his kitchen remodeling team home so I can write in peace and quiet. Instead, I decided to use this slogan and took personal action to limit the disruption. This way of viewing things saved me a lot of aggravation and was a more realistic approach in that situation. This won't last forever, and preserving the relationship with my neighbor is more important in the bigger scheme of things.

When we can't change the world, we can change our response.

This brings me right to my next slogan. Identifying steps I can take in this noisy neighbor situation helps me to remain optimistic and positive throughout the kitchen renovation. It _is_ going to happen and is already here now, so all I can do is change my reaction to mitigate the inconvenience. Options in this example include earplugs, music via earbud, closing doors, and moving to areas that are less noisy.

I could even go to a library if it was unbearable. Luckily, it's not, but I do think I will go get those earbuds and put on some nice binaural beats while I work. My silver lining thought right now is the optimistic thought that this is day three of the project and it's a small kitchen.

Give yourself a pat on the back (for your efforts).

While it might seem like something small to be able to take care of my needs (the earbuds did the trick), it is important that I give myself kudos for resolving the challenge in a way that meets my needs rather than stewing about it. Any chance you get to say "bravo" for a job well done at remaining positive in the face of adversity should be taken. Boosting your sense of mastery as you build your ability to leverage TOC Talk is important, particularly if you have spent many years letting events beyond your control dictate your mood.

You can change your mood by moving your body.

As mentioned, I could have gotten out of the house to get away from the kitchen racket had I chosen to go this route. When you feel upset about both large and small circumstances, moving your body can be very helpful. We have already briefly discussed that dance is one way to change your state, in addition to music.

Physical activity, even moving from one room to another, can be valuable when it comes to instantly changing your mood. If you are unable to get moving with your body, you can do this with a quick shift of focus. I sometimes use puzzles or videos of cute animals to shift my attention when my mood dips and I can't get out and about. Don't forget the Sunshine Gaze key from Chapter 2.

Worrying about this is wasted energy (that could be put to better use).

If you are prone to worrying, you are not alone. Many people who lean toward emotional sensitivity like I do are genetically wired for neurotic thinking patterns. I was elated when I found out this is not a disease, but rather a personality trait. Nevertheless, worry can wreak havoc on your optimism levels if you aren't careful.

While assessing circumstances in your life for decision-making can be valuable, chronic rumination when situations cannot be immediately resolved, or circumstances are beyond your control, can suck you dry. When you are weighing your options and ruminating about things, sometimes the best decision is to decide not to decide. You can choose to use the various techniques throughout this book to modify your mindset instead. As soon as you realize you are spending too much effort trying to solve the unsolvable, try this slogan as a reminder that your energy is a valuable commodity you can't afford to expend.

Use humor and comedy (to make yourself feel better).

I literally just laughed out loud because I moved to the other side of my place, put the earbuds on with the binaural beats, closed the doors, and suddenly the kitchen crew decided to use some sort of loud construction equipment that easily penetrated all of my solutions to the disruptive noise. I shifted to comedy because I could choose to laugh (which is medicine for the soul) at the irony or disrupt my joy by getting angry. Luckily, they have stopped now, but it was pretty funny.

In my former life, this situation might have sent me into a frenzy of self-pity or wild frustration. Not today. Today my focus was on the irony of doing all of these proactive things *while writing about it* and still being disrupted. Imagine if I were watching a skit or short comedy show about someone else. It would be hysterically comical. It kind of reminds me of a Seinfeld episode.

You can only control your inner self, not the outer world.

While this might seem obvious, I have met many people who spin their wheels regularly trying to manipulate outer situations in order to make life perfect. If you haven't come across the The Untethered Soul by Michael A. Singer, this is a good read. Particularly if you find yourself constantly looking to the external world to make you happy. While a nice new sports car can bring you temporary joy, it is outside of you and will not ultimately solve your problems.

Focusing on your inner peace without relying on changing your environment with stuff is something that takes practice. The society we live in tends to be fairly materialistic. Knowing when it's time to get a new job, new relationship, or new home takes discernment.

As you know from the stories I have told, it took me many years to realize that I take myself with me no matter what I grasp for in my outer world. Today my focus is much more on changing my inner thoughts and feelings rather than trying to manipulate the world around me to make me feel good.

You have a right to feel this way (without guilt).

Validating ourselves for how we feel about situations is as important as recognizing that feelings come and go. No matter what, it's important to cut yourself slack when you are upset about something. Whether the way you feel is rational or not, it's how you feel. If you change your thoughts, sometimes your feelings will follow, but sometimes they will not. Allowing yourself grace without guilting yourself out about it is important. You are a human being, not an artificial intelligence (AI) bot. Cut yourself some slack and give yourself permission.

As a child, I wasn't "allowed" to get angry. It was against the rules. Now, I remind myself that if I am angry, whether for a good reason or due to a distorted viewpoint, it's okay to have the emotion without making myself wrong or bad.

It's a brief moment. (You'll get over it and feel better in time.)

No matter what happens, events that are not what you wanted or envisioned, please remember that you will not stay upset forever. Life has ups and downs. Obviously, some situations are more serious than others but even the death of a family member or a life-altering accident, while terribly tragic, will not keep you perpetually down in the dumps, particularly once you are committed to a life filled with optimism.

There are many other slogans that I teach clients during live sessions or you can even make up your own, but this will get you started. Clichés can be used as well. They are similar to slogans, but rather than being specific to The Optimism Code, they are commonly known phrases you may have heard or read elsewhere. For example, the phrase, "When life hands you lemons, make lemonade" is based on a quote by Dale Carnegie, a well-known creator of self-improvement, sales, and corporate training programs.

🔑 TOC Keys: Helpful Clichés

There are so many wise sayings that have been passed along over the years, and their survival as "wise sayings" is due to their value. You can use clichés right alongside slogans whenever you need a quick phrase to combat negative thinking.

Below are a handful of clichés I have adopted as part of my own TOC Talk and shared with clients over the years.

1. ***You never fail until you stop trying.***

    When I lived in the West Indies, I made beaded jewelry. My business partner said someone requested a new design I had never created before. At first, I balked, but then he said, "You never fail until you stop trying," and I haven't forgotten it since. I went on to create a unique, one-of-a-kind necklace design. This mantra has gotten me through a myriad of challenges since that time. It helps maintain tenacity, so I don't give up without ensuring I have tried my best.

2. 🔑 *This, too, shall pass.*

I used to hate this one. My father would use this a lot when I was upset about one thing or the other as a teenager. Whether I was worried about a newly found zit or my best friend was spending time with her boyfriend instead of me, I was told, "This too shall pass," meaning the situation will not last forever. As a hypersensitive teenager, I didn't "get it," but now I do. It's all about perspective. You may notice that this phrase is very similar to the TOC slogan "It's a brief moment." Feel free to use them on your keychain interchangeably if you prefer this one.

3. 🔑 *Whatever doesn't kill you makes you stronger.*

This well-worn phrase sounds horrible on the surface, but it can be beneficial, particularly when you have lived through a traumatic experience. Wallowing in self-pity and feeling like a victim all the time is counterproductive. Sometimes, the events in our lives that are the most horrid turn out to be opportunities to strengthen us in ways we never imagined.

4. 🔑 *There is a solution to every problem.*

This was a saying that my ex-husband liked. His father, from Havana, Cuba, used to say, "There is a solution to every problem, but you may not always like the solution." I think of this when struggling with computer issues, which can be frustrating. Due to technical glitches, I have had to wipe out data on more than one occasion. Can you relate? I didn't like doing it, but it ultimately solved the problem. While you may not always get the result you are looking for in the timing you want, evaluating situations that might require a pivot in the face of adversity can be valuable.

5. 🔑 *When life hands you lemons, make lemonade.*

How we remedy "sticky" situations matters. I used to play the victim and cling to what I didn't want. Now, I recognize that I only have one choice: to make the best of a "not so great" situation as quickly as possible. Looking at the sweeter side of seemingly sour events is the very definition of optimism.

6. 🔑 *The universe has my back.*

While this is the last cliché I have chosen to include in The Optimism Code, it is one of my favorite sayings. I often use it as a form of gratitude when things go my way, and I also say it when I am in the midst of a challenge to remind myself that everything will work out for my greater good. I find it very comforting.

As you listen to your own self-talk this week, try to identify any clichés, either positive or negative, you may already be using without realizing it. Depending upon where you live geographically and what your heritage is, it's possible you have picked up a variety of sayings without even realizing it. Identify the helpful phrases and transform those that are less-than-ideal by adding one of the TOC slogans or a traditional cliché any time you catch yourself with stinkin' thinkin'.

TOC Talk: Three Questions to Ask Yourself

1. What was the event or circumstance that got you upset?

As you identify what upset you, try to be factual and brief so you don't get sidetracked. This is a "what happened?" question.

2. What thoughts ran through your head, and what sort of bodily stress response did you have?

This second question is more specific to what you thought about what happened. This is where mindfulness is important, as sometimes thoughts can be under the surface. Paying attention to your thinking in the moment is valuable. Also notice the physiological reactions you have or had during the initial trigger.

3. What slogans or clichés did you say to calm yourself and look at things with more optimism?

If you haven't used any yet, that's okay. You can do this by asking yourself the three questions. "I've provided space on for this on the next page." Notice how you feel after you are done with this exercise and feel free to repeat it as necessary.

_____

_____

_____

As with any language, learning TOC Talk takes time; whether you are adopting new slogans or memorizing clichés you were previously unfamiliar with. Once you start repeating these phrases to yourself regularly, they become increasingly automated. You may even find that your newfound "optimism language" rubs off on those around you, so don't be afraid to share a few of these with your friends, relatives, and coworkers. While you may have inadvertently automated negative self-talk undermining your desire to live with greater optimism, you can now redirect your thoughts using TOC Talk going forward.

In addition to using slogans and clichés to combat negative thinking and reduce your stress and anxiety, affirmations and additional reframing techniques can go a long way in boosting your self-esteem and reducing life's daily upsets. In our next chapter, we will explore the value of realistically worded affirmations and discuss the secrets to re-framers, which are stories you can make up for fun to cope better with unpleasant situations you may not have the power to change.

OPTIMISM DECODER

Chapter 6
Creating Your Own TOC Talk:
The Language of Optimism

- Negative messaging passed down through generations can be counteracted with a variety of positive self-talk strategies.

- TOC Talk is a strategy to reprogram the brain with positive self-talk and counteract negative thinking patterns.

- Asking yourself specific questions using a 3-step method will help you memorize the slogans and cliches of TOC Talk.

- You can think of TOC Talk as a language that must be learned and reinforced until you become fluent.

- Your brain will automate TOC Talk with practice which will help to reduce stress and anxiety.

https://theoptimismcode.com

Chapter 7

Defining Yourself and Your World with Max Positivity

"Any idea, plan, or purpose may be placed in the mind through repetition of thought."

Napoleon Hill

Your mind is powerful. Imagining a future filled with joy and optimism can help you on your way. Right now, take a moment to envision yourself super happy and successful. What are you wearing? What do you look like? How do you feel? Who are you with? Hold that image in your head for 20-30 seconds, describing it to yourself.

Think of affirmations as a way to rebrand yourself. For example, maybe you were told you were big-boned in your youth, and now, years later, you feel insecure about your body and say critical things to yourself. Affirmations can help you redefine yourself in a kinder way.

While saying nice things to yourself often may seem odd at first, it's an extremely effective way to boost optimism. Whether you want to get rid of habits, improve your health, boost self-esteem, or increase your earnings, affirmations can be a big help. When done properly, positive affirmations can override negative beliefs for good, turning your brain into a positivity machine. I absolutely love using positive affirmations and have had great results in my own life. I enjoy watching people I coach transform as well. When used properly, it's like witnessing a miracle when affirmations are correctly used

IMPORTANT: Affirmation Guidelines

It's important to phrase your affirmations using "I *am*," or, "You *are*," statements for maximum effectiveness. "I *am* a wonderful person," for example. Or, you could say, "You *are* a wonderful person," as if you are getting this information from someone else. If saying a phrase like this to yourself right now feels disingenuous, you can start with a modified version. "I am *becoming* a wonderful person," is bound to give you more optimism than "I *am* a bad seed." If you can believe it, my mother, may she rest in peace, used to say this about me. She thought it was funny. Me—not so much.

By putting your affirmative statement in the present tense, you can act as if it's already true until you start believing it. Some affirmations will resonate with you more than others, so don't be afraid to play around with them and even create new ones to address various areas of your life.

🔑 TOC Keys: Positive Affirmations

While affirmations are simple, following a set of guidelines is helpful as you make them your own. I recommend taking advantage of the same "Good, Better, Best" approach we explored in forming a gratitude habit. Small steps are the way to go regarding habit formation if you tend to fizzle out when attempting larger goals.

Good

Listen to positive affirmation audio/videos daily for 21 days.

Better

Write down five to seven positive affirmations daily for at least 21 days, preferably longer.

Best

Listen to positive affirmation audio/videos AND write down ten positive affirmations daily for at least 30 days.

Counteracting Past Programming

As I just pointed out, positive affirmations are a great way to counterbalance negative programming you may have received in childhood. Most people I know have picked up some form of negative messaging that can be turned around using this technique.

I could have gone with a positive statement that addressed "the bad seed" and started saying, "I *am* a good seed," but I instead went with statements like, "I *am* an awesome human being," and, "I am a wonderful and special person." While these may sound a little conceited at first blush, I smile every time I think of myself in this loving way and no longer think of myself as bad. Imperfect, absolutely, but a bad seed, absolutely not. I genuinely believe in my value and recognize that my mother did not intend to scar me with her *special* nickname.

Habit Reversal

Positive affirmations are great for habit reversal, too. Let's say you are a smoker and want to quit. You have a current identity now. "I *am* a smoker" is what you tell yourself and others. Now, if you don't really want to quit, this will not work, but let's assume you really and truly do want to quit smoking. You can create an affirmation like. "I *am* a non-smoker," or, "You *are* a non-smoker." For emphasis and to make it more realistic, you might want to throw in the word "now" at the end of your phrase. "I *am* a non-smoker now."

Alternatively, you could make it about today and state, "I *am* a non-smoker (or ex-smoker) today." You could even say, "I *am* an ex-smoker. I used to smoke, but I quit." You could embellish your positive affirmation by adding more detail as well. "I *am* proud I quit smoking," or, "I *am* feeling great now that I *am* no longer a smoker." By adding some additional "story" to your affirmation, you will prime yourself to begin thinking this way. This technique can be used to aid in breaking a variety of habits as long as you are on a mission to do so. If you are ambivalent and don't really want to change your behavior, even the most well-structured affirmations will not be 100% effective.

Self-Esteem Brain Boosts

Positive affirmations have tremendous power to transform your self-identity. They are easy to overlay on top of negative mantras, so as long as you are done clinging to a past identity that isn't serving you well, they will work. I already mentioned, "I am an awesome human being," and, "I am a wonderful and special person." Here are a few other positive affirmations my clients have used successfully in their journey toward greater optimism. Feel free to go with the "You are" approach or even sets of both "I *am*," and, "You *are*," as you build your list of positive phrases.

🔑 I am a beautiful person.

🔑 I am worthy and loved.

🔑 I am important in the world.

🔑 I am valuable and needed.

🔑 I am an awesome human being.

🔑 I am getting better and becoming an amazing person day by day.

Can you think of one or two positive affirmations using, "I am," or "You are," that resonate with you and might counteract past negative beliefs?

_____

_____

Daily Affirmations With Stuart Smalley

Years ago, there was a Saturday Night Live skit with Stuart Smalley where he said, "I'm good enough, I'm smart enough, and doggone it, people like me." Stuart hosted a fictional self-help show that poked fun at this method. While it is comical, I can personally attest that if you repeat affirmations consistently and keep your phrasing positive, you will likely get outstanding optimism-boosting results.

Remember, when creating positive affirmations, it's important to avoid inadvertently veering toward the negative. If you catch yourself using phrases like, "I don't" or "I no longer" be sure to course correct as soon as possible. Focus on what you are going toward rather than what you are going away from.

Future Goal Attainment & Law of Attraction (LOA)

In addition to helping with habits and self-esteem, positive affirmations can manifest success in sales, weight loss, romance, job search, and more. The law of attraction is always present, even when we attract what we don't want. As we say things to ourselves, we reinforce the direction of our lives. If you were raised by parents who saw money as being very scarce, for example, you might believe that money doesn't grow on trees, it takes money to make money, or only college-educated people can get ahead.

These overarching beliefs can manifest as limitations. Once you understand that you have been manifesting your circumstances on some level, you will be in a position to transform your mindset. Often, these beliefs lie under the surface without our awareness. It is a worthwhile exercise to make a list of statements that may be holding you back in finances, career, health, and relationships.

If where you want to go is being thwarted by past programming, it is time to create a new vision for your future and imagine a limitless world where you get everything you want. While some say you can use this technique to manifest a great parking spot, I like to use it for slightly more important transformations.

Obviously, if you are 5'1", you are unlikely to become a successful basketball player, so LOA has limitations, but reaching for the stars, so to speak, has value. Imagine if you want a happy and healthy relationship with your spouse, but lately, you have been arguing a lot. You could create an image of the two of you holding hands, enjoying a vacation together, or embracing in a passionate kiss.

In addition to the image, add some positive affirmations about your relationship. Feel free to use, "We *are*," to describe how you and your mate get along. For example, "We *are* madly in love. We *get along* super well now."

You could link your vision of the future to deep breathing or other mindfulness practices like traditional meditation. Focusing daily on your desires and goals for the future will get you one step closer. Athletes and billionaires have used the Law of Attraction to manifest success.

As mentioned, I have included a resources section at the end of this book that links to the Optimism Code website. Here, you can find recommendations for content on positive affirmations, manifestation, and other techniques for creating a life filled with maximum joy.

🔑 TOC Key: Re-framers

Re-framers are a little different than the other TOC Talk Keys. Changing how you frame the situations and events in your life can be very valuable, even when the reframing is not based on reality. I want to give you a funny example of how I used the reframing technique to feel better about a circumstance beyond my control. I have a neighbor named Joe. Joe is a wonderful person, and we get along great. He is friendly and usually very quiet.

However, he and I have doors that open directly across from one another. When I need to get deliveries left in the hallway, there is a possibility he will see me, whether I am appropriately dressed or not. Joe has a quirky habit of leaving his door open a crack. I once asked him why he does this. He originally said it was because he was listening out for a neighbor who lived next door and was in ill health… but that individual is no longer living there, and he still does this bizarre behavior.

At first, I let it bother me because it made me feel like he might open his door any second. On some level, I allowed it to interfere with my sense of privacy. Whenever I opened my door and saw his ever so slightly ajar, I thought, *Hasn't he seen any episodes of Forensic Files? Why would he do such a thing?* The bottom line is that I let it bug me at first. Then, I decided to use a re-framer, and since that time, it hasn't bothered me in the least.

I made up a story to reframe his quirky behavior. My made-up theory is that he was once in a fire, and leaving his door open a crack helps him feel better about getting out safely. I can almost guarantee this reframing is not true, but it works for me. I now view his door-ajar habit as something helpful for him, and my attitude has completely softened. I still find it odd, but having personally been in a building on fire, I find this tall tale resonates with me. At the time, I was living in Manhattan, and apparently, someone on a lower floor fell asleep with a lit cigarette. The fire escape led to a blocked back area, and I had to wait until the firefighters put the blaze out before being ushered through the building to safety. I still become alert whenever I smell smoke.

By using a re-framer, I was able to transform my annoyance at Joe into compassion. While I would strongly prefer him to close his door properly, telling myself he is doing it because of past trauma helps me to cope in a way that lends itself to forgiveness and understanding rather than resentment. I have helped many clients through challenging situations, including illness, divorce, and job loss, by teaching them how to re-frame things in a way that just feels better using similar mind tricks.

Let's say you were in a competition and lost. You were up for an award, but someone else got the glory. You know that your work was better than theirs, or at least you believe this to be true. Let's even say that it was obvious the judges favored your competitor, and you got a raw deal. You could spend the rest of your life angry about this or create a fun re-framer.

Maybe you could go to a trophy store, get a special trophy, and have it engraved to say, "Best Runner Up." This might not do the trick, but it's one idea. Perhaps you could make up a story like I did and assume that this person needed the trophy more than you because they came from a broken home or were recently divorced. The sky's the limit on what you can come up with to feel better.

It doesn't matter if the story you make up is real or not. Don't be afraid to get creative when it comes to re-framers. They are inventions of your mind designed to alleviate upset and anxiety. Re-framers don't need to be based on factual data. All that matters is that they make you feel better.

Another example could be when your best friend is late for a lunch you planned months ago. He or she hasn't shown up, and you are wondering what happened. Make up a soothing story. They got stuck in traffic. They had the wrong day. They lost their cell phone. Any re-framer you can make up that works to calm you in the moment will work. Eventually, you will find out what happened, but why work yourself up wondering what occurred when you can go on your merry way with joy by reframing the situation? Learning how to do this takes a little practice, but it pays off by preventing unnecessary agitation when things don't go as you would like.

I realize that there is a lot to unpack between this chapter and the last. In Chapter 9, things will come together more clearly, so you can practice some of these TOC strategies and make them your own. The biggest takeaway from this chapter is to remember that your thoughts are extremely important when it comes to maintaining optimism. It all starts with paying attention to what you are saying to yourself.

By directing your thoughts in a positive way and course correcting as needed, you hold the keys to self-empowerment. As you assemble the keys to transform what you say to yourself, it can make all the difference in the world regarding your well-being.

OPTIMISM DECODER

Chapter 7
Defining Yourself and Your World
with Max Positivity

- We all pick up negative messages from those around us when we are children, or even as adults.

- Using affirmations is a great strategy for rewriting your history and creating a new "brand" for yourself that is more positive.

- Positive affirmations using "I AM" and "You ARE" statements can transform self-identity and help you eliminate bad habits.

- Law of Attraction (LOA) can be used with affirmations to manifest success in various areas of your life.

- Reframing techniques referred to as re-framers provide you with a method for transforming your perspective when you are met with challenging situations.

https://theoptimismcode.com

Chapter 8

The M Word: Let's Talk about Meditation Options

"You have power over your mind – not outside events. Realize this, and you will find strength."

Marcus Aurelius

When I started to meditate formally, I thought the incessant chatter in my head was due to some defect in my mind. Back then, if I could last more than 15 seconds without shifting from past to present to future and back again, I considered myself lucky. But then I learned to stop judging and criticizing myself for not being able to concentrate, and overnight, my meditation got a whole lot easier.

Since this time, I have come to realize I am not alone. It is not a personal defect to have stray thoughts while meditating. It is completely normal. Whether you have struggled with meditating or are an avid meditator, accepting the wandering mind is part of the process. Instead of chastising yourself when your mind strays, recognize you haven't been present and bring yourself back to the moment. The act of redirecting your focus is one of the benefits of meditation.

In addition to calming my mind, meditation allows me to experience my fully alert moments with greater awareness and joy. Bringing your attention back to the moment is invaluable when it comes to maximizing optimism. Now, when I catch myself dwelling on the past or worrying about the future, all I need to do is focus on what is happening in the moment. It's an amazing superpower.

Which Type of Meditation is Best?

Choosing from the many different meditation methods available can often be confusing.

While the non-meditation mindfulness (aka NMM) techniques I shared with you in Chapter 5 are great, deeper meditation practices can potentially do more to build your prefrontal cortex so you can get control of the monkey mind. With practice, refocusing your attention gets much easier. As you gain greater ability to decide what you focus on, your optimism levels will rise exponentially.

I have explored a variety of meditation methods over the years. Having benefited from Mantra Meditation, Mindfulness-Based Stress Reduction (MBSR), Yoga Nidra, and more, I find it nice to have options. Each type of meditation has its nuances. The answer to which meditation is best is truly a personal one. For me, it has morphed over time and can even change day to day depending upon my mood, my privacy levels, and my schedule.

When to Meditate

My time is the morning, as I find my mind is less busy and can bring myself into the present moment more easily. I have paired my meditation with my morning routine, which has become second nature. I am an early bird, though, and recognize the morning approach is not for everyone. Some of my clients with sleep challenges have found that meditating right before they go to bed or when they wake up in the middle of the night is helpful. Others meditate successfully during their lunch hour or a short break. Meditation can be done for as little as one minute or as long as one hour plus. My sweet spot is about 25 minutes, but 15 minutes or even five will do the trick when time-pressed.

If you are new to meditation, start slowly and work your way up. Try out different types of meditation to see which ones you like. If, along the way, you find a method that resonates with you, use it. You can always explore other approaches down the line. You don't have to meditate daily, but making a steady habit of it is a good idea for consistent results. When I have extra time on the weekend, I take advantage of this and extend my meditation session accordingly.

The Many Types of Meditation

While I am not going to go through every single type of meditation, I will focus on the ones that are simple, easy, and effective. Meditation has been practiced for centuries by many different cultures. You may have an image of someone seated in the lotus position with their thumb and index fingers together in a ring chanting "lak-lak-lak-lak," but as you will learn, this is not the only way to practice meditation. It can be done lying down, sitting in an office chair, or even on a park bench.

Guided Meditation

Guided meditation is probably one of the easiest forms and can be done sitting up or lying down. The beauty of guided meditation is that you passively listen to someone telling you to imagine scenery, which can direct your focus to their voice. The downside is that some people have a harder time with visualization than others.

Visualization

Visualization meditation is a form of guided meditation that can help manifest the future. For example, athletes have effectively used this technique to imagine themselves performing perfectly. We learn differently, so some people will respond well to auditory suggestions telling them to imagine themselves walking on a beach in their ideal body, while others will get limited benefits.

MBSR

MBSR, which stands for Mindfulness-Based Stress Reduction, is arguably one of the most well-studied forms of guided meditation out there and has been used for everything from managing post-traumatic stress disorder (PTSD) to alleviating chronic pain. I am fortunate to have participated in a comprehensive program focused on MBSR and was able to learn many foundational principles that help me to this day, no matter which form of meditation I am doing. In particular, my ability to ignore outside sounds while meditating has improved tremendously, so distractions don't get in my way.

Dr. Joe Dispenza Meditation

While I find MBSR very valuable and love that it has been heavily researched, my personal favorites are the Joe Dispenza meditations. Some of them are a little woo-woo (out there), but I appreciate that they combine binaural beats (discussed in Chapter 5) with guided imagery. Dr. Joe Dispenza's story is quite fascinating as well. When he was a chiropractor, Dr. Joe got hit by a truck while biking and was told to get back surgery, but instead, he developed his own approach to healing. It worked, and since then, he has written multiple books and developed various programs focused on leveraging quantum physics and neuroscience in the context of healing.

My go-to when I am time-pressed is the Dr. Joe free Hay House audio, which can be found at the time of this writing on most podcast services and is a little over 15 minutes long. It's called *Guided Space Meditation*. I remember, when I first heard it, thinking it was way too weird because of the space references, but I went with it and kept at it.

While it doesn't happen every time I listen to Dr. Joe's meditations, I have been fortunate to experience a complete numbing sensation throughout my body that has been nothing short of a miracle when I'm in pain. I could write so much more about this style of meditation as well as his background. While I plan to blog about it in the future, for now, so we can stay on point, I will leave it to you to research further.

Chakra Meditation

Chakra meditation focuses on the seven energy centers within the body and may include deep breathing, yoga poses, and visualizations. Dr. Joe has a variant he calls *Blessings of the Energy Centers* and there are several videos and audios on the Internet that can explain more about this ancient practice rooted in Hindu philosophy and spirituality.

Singing Bowl Meditation

Tibetan singing bowls originated in the Himalayas thousands of years ago and have been used in multiple Asian cultures and now in the West. The soothing sounds reverberate and can help promote relaxation, calming the mind to reduce stress and anxiety, decrease pain, improve sleep, and even boost immune function. This form of meditation has been associated with mood enhancements.

In my city, some people come together to enjoy singing bowl meditation, but you can also put your earbuds in and enjoy the sounds and vibes online. While I am no expert in singing bowls, I find the sounds have a similar effect to binaural beats and can be very healing. Give 'em a try. All you have to do is listen and focus on the music. Singing bowls can also be played as background music while you work or during a lunch break.

Mantra Meditation

I was first introduced to Mantra meditation during a course I enrolled in with Deepak Chopra. I learned an ancient Sanskrit phrase that I repeated over and over again. I paired this with an audio of binaural beats, and it crowded out all other thoughts. Many people like mantra meditation, and you don't have to use Sanskrit to get benefits. You can just as easily repeat a phrase like peace, calm, or well-being to keep thoughts from entering your mind. You can even pair your mantra with a breathing exercise if you like.

Staring Meditation

I previously mentioned sitting on the porch with my mom, waiting for my dad to come home, and staring at the bushes. Mom called it contemplating. Whether you focus on a candle or a point on the wall, staring meditation, also referred to as Trataka, can be a powerful and effective way to relax your mind.

All you need to do is maintain your focus on one point. In addition to improving concentration, it can help you to feel more peaceful. One of my favorite ways of practicing Trataka is staring at the embers and dancing flames in a fireplace. I find it incredibly soothing.

Yoga Nidra | iRest

While Yoga Nidra (also known as iRest) sounds like it would be yoga, which can be beneficial as well, it is a method that incorporates many different meditation ideologies. The creator, Richard Miller, PhD, spent time reviewing the best of the best to develop this unique process, which can produce deep levels of relaxation and reduce anxiety. In addition, Yoga Nidra iRest can be beneficial to pain sufferers and those with PTSD.

During a session, you are invited to get as comfortable as possible in whatever position feels best and then switch focus from one area of your body to another, assessing without judgment. There is a free app called Mindfulness Coach that was made for the US Veterans Administration (VA), where you can download iRest meditations. It is available on both Android and iPhone.

There are also trained Yoga Nidra instructors if you prefer live support. My only complaint about Yoga Nidra is that, generally, music isn't included with the meditations, and I prefer to add sound. That said, this is a powerful method of meditation that helped me develop the ability to focus my attention at will. I encourage you to explore it further.

Walking Meditation

Technically, walking meditation could be considered a non-meditation mindfulness technique because you are moving when you do it, but I chose to include it in this mindfulness section rather than in Chapter 5 because, when done correctly, it can immerse you in an amazing experience with profound benefits. I have used Dr. Joe Dispenza's walking meditation available on his website for purchase. At times I have been able to experience a whole hour or more of focused attention on my surroundings. I have also simply started walking and blended a series of mindfulness practices together to achieve results.

While I always observe nature with gratitude and mindfulness, I enjoy walking meditation when I am completely attentive in the moment, literally acting as an observer. By paying attention in real-time to the most minor details, from a crack in the road to the nuances of a brightly colored flower, I get a profound sense of joy with my entire being in the present moment for an extended period.

While you don't have to do a walking meditation exactly the way I do, you can take a brief walk in the morning or on a break and pay attention to your breathing as you do so. Noticing your environment in great detail and repeatedly bringing your monkey mind back to the moment can do wonders to boost your mood. Here is a TOC Key to give you a taste of what a walking meditation is like.

🔑 TOC Key: 2 Minute Mindfulness Walk

This two-minute mindfulness walk can be done outdoors or inside, depending upon your time availability and personal environment.

1. From a standing position, start by taking a deep breath through your nose and releasing it through your mouth.

2. Begin observing your regular breathing pattern now without doing anything other than following the air in and out. Listen to the sound, notice the sensation, and follow your breath for a bit, focusing on only this moment.

3. Next, take a first step forward, focusing on your feet as you move very slowly forward.

4. As you look down at your feet, notice the color and texture of the floor beneath you. Pay attention to your shoes or socks. If you are barefoot, notice your toes hitting the ground as you move forward.

5. Silently name the colors and objects in your field of vision without judging them. If you are outside, it could be a green tree, yellow car, blue sky, purple flowers, white fence, tan bench, and so on. If you are inside, you might think to yourself, *blue wall, clear window, brown flooring, silver ceiling fan, wooden computer desk,* etc.

6. Notice the sounds around you and the feeling of the air touching your skin. If you want to, you can also name those sounds and sensations. Cool, hot, breezy, people talking, dog barking, telephone ringing, etc. This will keep you focused on what is happening now.

7. You can also shift your attention back to breathing if your mind strays. If you have started thinking about anything besides your mindfulness walk, bring yourself back to the present moment.

8. Now, stop walking and lift your lower arms upward until they are at a 90-degree angle. Turn your palms upward,

holding your fingers loosely as if you are cradling a light ping-pong ball.

9. Next, breathe deeply through your nose, hold it, smile, and breathe out slowly through your mouth.

10. That's it. You just meditated. Congratulate yourself. How do you feel now versus two minutes ago?

See how easy that was? If you were unable to follow the instructions perfectly, no biggie. The point of this exercise is to give you an easy flavor of what meditating for even two minutes can do for you. If you have mobility issues and are unable to do this exercise fully, you can still benefit by doing some of the other steps outlined in this exercise.

I recognize this is a lot of information to take in. While I haven't covered every single type of meditation there is, I hope this broad overview has given you a glimpse of what is possible so you can pick and choose a mindfulness method or two that will work for you.

In the next chapter, we will cover various ways you can optimize your brain and body health to improve optimism levels and release more feel-good chemicals. With targeted nutrition and supplementation, as well as regular physical movement and avoidance of environmental toxins, you can stack the cards in your favor when alleviating stress and anxiety. In the next chapter, I will also provide you with suggestions to improve sleep. Read on!

OPTIMISM DECODER

Chapter 8
The M Word: Let's Talk about Meditation Options

- Formal meditation can help you tame your "inner monkey mind" and show it who's boss.

- Knowing it's normal for your mind to wander will help you to prevent frustration as you master different techniques.

- Meditation doesn't have to be complicated and can be done for only one or two minutes while still providing benefits.

- There are many different meditation methods worth exploring to find out what works best for you.

- Regular meditation has been linked to reductions in stress and anxiety, inner calm, and improvements in well-being.

https://theoptimismcode.com

Chapter 9

Priming Your Body for a Healthier Mind in an Insane World

"To keep the body in good health is a duty... otherwise we shall not be able to keep our mind strong and clear."

Buddha

When your mind is clear and your body is well taken care of, it's much easier to maintain higher levels of optimism. I can personally attest to this, as better health significantly impacts my overall sense of joy.

Unfortunately, if you're chronically stressed, it is easy to forget the importance of caring for your body. Maybe you reach for foods that soothe in the moment, or you ditch your exercise routine. Next thing you know, you're struggling with sleep. I truly understand how this can happen because it has happened to me.

🔑 Eat Real Food

I will start with the most obvious dietary recommendations I can. Good nutrition begins with eating real, unprocessed foods. Real food is key, so add it to your keychain. Sadly, as I was getting my list together for a run to the supermarket this morning, I was looking at the sale items and estimated that roughly 80% of the "buy one, get one" items belong in a category I call fake foods.

I define 'fake foods' as items made in a factory that contain ingredients you and I would not find in nature. This is a pretty lengthy list nowadays. The good news is that most of us still have wide availability of foods that are whole, real, and nutritious in our grocery stores. For this, I am grateful.

I have spent a long time observing how my body works best and have noticed that my outlook is more optimistic, in general, when I am feeling well-nourished with real foods that are not too high in fiber. Perhaps you, like me, have tried different food approaches. Whole foods, ketogenic, vegetarian, fasting, etc. I've learned that my body functions better when I regulate my carbs and eat less often, avoiding snacking to give my digestive system a rest. The fuel I put in my body definitely affects how I feel.

One of the best things I did that made a huge difference in the context of eating whole foods was to eliminate nearly all foods made with flour and sugar. My clients who have successfully drawn this same line in the sand report mood improvements. If you have been eating an industrialized diet, it is worth looking at what you can do to make some positive changes. I am a member of The Fasting Method and also avoid snacking. Regarding your specific dietary choices, nutrition is very personal, so I will leave it at that for now.

🔑 Brain Power Supplements

Similarly, the choice to take supplements is very individual. I want to introduce you to several specific products you may find helpful when it comes to optimizing brain health. While not mandatory, supplements can be valuable aids toward alleviating stress and anxiety as well as improving cognition and concentration. Please proceed with caution and consult your healthcare provider. If you get the green light, select brands of the highest quality, even if they cost a bit more. Look for products made using good manufacturing practices (GMP) that ideally mention third-party testing.

1. **Phosphatidylcholine**—While it can be pricey and hard to pronounce, phosphatidylcholine is known for improving cognition, memory, and overall brain function.

2. **Phosphatidylserine**—Similar to phosphatidylcholine, this is classified as a phospholipid. It may help you modulate high cortisol levels, which can potentially interfere with sleep and cause you to feel jittery.

3. **Ashwagandha**—Among its benefits, Ashwagandha seems to improve executive function in the brain, quieting the monkey mind, and may also reduce stress and anxiety.

4. **L-Theanine**—Found in green and black tea, this amino acid is said to promote sleep and relaxation. Because it can potentially lower blood pressure, be sure to take this into consideration when supplementing.

5. **Omega 3s**—EPA and DHA are essential fatty acids linked to improved mood regulation and cognitive function. We typically get too many Omega 6s and not enough Omega 3s in our diet. Also, freshness matters greatly with this supplement, so choose wisely and refrigerate after opening.

6. **Inositol**—This supplement, which is also present in foods we eat, seems to help regulate brain function at the cellular level and is involved in maintaining the connections within our nervous system.

7. **Magnesium**—There are many forms of magnesium, and some are better than others when it comes to brain support. L-Threonate is able to cross the blood-brain barrier and may improve sleep while reducing stress and anxiety. Magnesium Taurate is another form that can be helpful for mood improvement. Epsom salt baths or lotions with Magnesium Sulfate aid in muscle relaxation.

There is so much more I could write about nutrition and supplements, but I will save this for my blog, or a future book. As with most of the topics I share, I have included a variety of links to helpful resources on The Optimism Code website linked at the end of this book.

🔑 Home and Personal Care Products

In addition to watching what you eat, I want to mention the impact environmental chemicals can have on hormonal regulation and mood. It's hard to get away from the many products on the market, but I try my best to limit the toxin load and avoid disrupting my endocrine system. It is a good idea to evaluate the household products you are using if you struggle with hormonal issues that you feel may be impacting your mindset.

I recommend looking at data from the not-for-profit group EWG for more information. It's worth assessing your food sources, cookware and storage containers, cleaning products, and personal care brands to consider ways to cut back on toxins that may have impacted your well-being. Regarding environmental considerations, reducing exposure is the name of the game since it's impossible to avoid everything. This is one more step you can take to safeguard brain health.

🔑 Movement & Physical Activity

In addition to aiding digestion and helping with blood sugar control, regular physical movement in some form or another is a great mood booster and can have many positive brain benefits. As you know by now, I am a huge fan of nature walks.

When I go for one of my morning strolls, I almost always rattle off ten things I am grateful for in seconds just by scanning my surroundings. I find walking to be one of the activities that enriches my life and makes me feel truly joyous. Today, I saw ponds, ducks, egrets, trees, flowers, dogs, bunnies, and more. I also got morning sunlight. Sadly, there are days my aches and pains get the best of me, and I also realize that not everyone is as lucky as I am as a Floridian to be able to walk regularly in a natural setting year-round. If you haven't been getting as much exercise as you feel you should, there are many avenues, no matter the limitations.

Precious Time

No law says you have to spend an hour on a treadmill. (Thank goodness! I would not like that law at all.) If you feel you can't find the time to do some, the good news is that you can start with the one-minute approach.

When I first started doing Zumba again after a hiatus due to foot pain, I put an online video on and danced for one minute, modifying my technique to prevent injury. Before I knew it, I was doing two minutes. The next thing I knew, I wanted to watch a second song, and before I knew it, I added small dumbbells to my dance routine for just 30 seconds.

Some activity is better than none. I recommend you use the "Good, Better, Best" approach and do what you can, even if it is just for five minutes. If it helps, put reminders around your home to make it easier to follow through. Scheduling it on your calendar can make it part of your routine. Even sitting at an office desk, a few isometric stomach crunches and leg lifts can be of value.

If you prefer to go to a gym or fitness class, figure out the day or days that might work for you and choose a location that is as convenient as possible. I love the cliché, "Don't let perfect be the enemy of good," when it comes to exercise. Making time to incorporate physical activity is essential for your emotional well-being. I know how easy it is to make excuses when you are busy or not feeling well, but movement is worth prioritizing for your happiness and health.

🔑 TOC Keys: Seated Exercises

Here is a brief example of a chair exercise routine you can complete in under five minutes a day, even if you are busy or suffer from chronic pain. It is based on isometrics, which don't require much movement but challenge your muscles. These exercises have been shown to improve mental health, benefit sleep, boost mood, and even reduce symptoms of post-traumatic stress disorder.

1. 🔑 **Stomach**—Sitting at a desk, chair, or car seat, breathe in through your nose and tighten your stomach muscles, counting down silently or out loud for five seconds. Breathe out through your mouth slowly, and you are done. Repeat five times, adding

one second to your count with each round until you reach 10.

2. 🔑 **Legs**—Starting with your feet flat on the floor in a seated position, lift your legs slightly upward while maintaining good posture and move your thighs slowly in so that your two knees come together and again out. Do this slowly and brace yourself with your arms if you need extra support. Repeat this inner-outer thigh motion 5-10 times. Feel free to do more repetitions if it feels comfortable to you.

If you are in a car (at a stop light, please), you can modify this and keep it 100% isometric by simply lifting your legs and holding. Be sure to put the car in park! You will engage your stomach again, but you want to try to include your leg muscles as well. This doesn't get the same exact muscles, but you will still get mindset benefits. My great aunt, who looked and felt amazing in her senior years, always used to do car exercises when stopped at traffic lights.

3. 🔑 **Arms**—As with the relaxation response discussed in Chapter 5, you can clench your fists into a tight ball and hold this for five seconds, then release for five seconds, and hold again for six seconds, and release for six seconds until you reach 10 seconds in total which will be five rounds. Feel free to combine this one with breath exercises as well.

There are many other seated exercises that can be done in a matter of minutes as one of your TOC Keys. If you already have a fitness routine, great, but if not, this routine can be a simple way to add some fitness to your life. I don't want anyone getting hurt on my watch, so consult with your healthcare provider if you have any limitations.

I just did a set of these exact seated exercises to time it, and it took me about three and a half minutes. I noticed a nice rush of feel-good chemicals that I assume was due to a rise in endorphins. It was well worth my time and effort as I use all the endorphins I can get for pain relief. Nice.

Even stretching can be very therapeutic if isometrics feel like a burden on any given day. Years ago, I was not a big fan of stretching. As I age, I find this form of movement very helpful, not only for blood flow and mental well-being, but to help alleviate discomfort.

Likes and Dislikes

If an exercise routine causes you to feel disgruntled, this is counterproductive to your goals. One way to make some exercises more enjoyable is to link them with your favorite music or an audiobook. Assess your thoughts and feelings to determine what forms of activity bring you the greatest pleasure, and never push through an exercise routine if you are in serious pain or discomfort. I once did a strenuous CrossFit workout that kept me from sitting down for days. Needless to say, I never went back!

Be mindful as you try different things out. If riding a stationary bike feels like slow torture, get off the bike and stretch, do some yoga, or walk in nature if you can. Mix it up to avoid boredom but try not to let your monkey mind tell you there's no time for a workout or you just don't *feel* like it. Sometimes, a minute is all you need to get started and kick in more enthusiasm. Focus on heading toward what works for you and listen to your inner voice so you can honor your needs.

Make a Pivot Plan

If you tell yourself you will walk and it rains, without a pivot plan, you may fall out of the habit. If you have the space at home, consider investing in fitness equipment you can use when inclement weather hits. Explore free online videos on a rainy day. It's your plan, so make it realistic for you and nobody else. When I work with clients one-on-one, we explore fitness options and create a workable strategy. I am constantly tweaking my own pivot plan to prioritize movement because I know it makes me feel better in general. Occasionally, I pivot to a resting day, too.

Sleep and Downtime

When swamped with to-dos, it's easy to forget to rest, but you really must. Burnout and illness loom large when you don't build downtime into your schedule. I recognize it can be a challenging balancing act when you have urgent obligations, but you may need to say no to a thing or two you would love to do to get adequate relaxation.

Avoiding Bright Lights

Whether you are staring at headlights on the road, LED billboards, or a cell phone screen, our world can easily prime you for sleep disruption. I use a clock with red digits and keep the setting low. I like screen dimming settings on my computer and my cell phones that work with my circadian rhythm to help me sleep better at night. Amber-tinted lenses can also be helpful when watching TV at night. You may want to invest in a good mask or some really good room-darkening curtains as

THE OPTIMISM CODE

well if you have challenges sleeping. Check out The Optimism Code resources for more suggestions.

You should shield your eyes from exposure to blue light at least a few hours before bedtime. When I go to nighttime events like hockey games or music concerts, I almost always have more fitful sleep because I am bombarded with bright lights that contain blue light. By becoming conscious of how light impacts your sleep, you can troubleshoot as necessary.

Soothing Sounds

I am in love with pink noise. Pink noise sounds similar to white noise and drowns out background sounds but tends to be more soothing. I find it less harsh. If you live in an area with sirens or are simply noise sensitive like me, consider options to drown out annoying background noise as much as possible. Having lived near an airport in the past, I know firsthand how anxiety-producing noise pollution can be.

As an aside, I just remembered a good re-framer I like to use when sirens go by. I tell myself they are rescuing someone, which is most often true. Suddenly, the annoying siren becomes a good thing rather than a net negative. I would like to be rescued by a noisy siren if I found myself in an emergency. Wouldn't you?

If you want to take this extra step when trying to sleep or relax, consider getting some good earplugs. My favorite and most comfortable kind are made from real wax and wrapped in cotton. Many people aren't comfortable wearing earplugs at night, but if you live in a densely populated area or have noisy neighbors, they are worth a try.

126

Morning Sunlight

Getting sunlight in the morning can be beneficial for night-time sleep. If you can step outside or onto a porch and glance toward the sun, this will allow the receptors in your eye to improve your circadian rhythm. I daily make an effort to look toward the sun but, of course, not directly into it. Even on cloudy days, I try to get morning light as I am not a sound sleeper in general and need all the help I can get. While I can get to sleep quite easily, I still have some challenges with staying asleep.

Mindset for Imperfect Sleep

If you are like me and have difficulty with sleep, it can be frustrating in the middle of the night. Between bathroom runs and tossing and turning to alleviate aches and pains, I have had some brutal nights. Don't even get me started on what it's like trying to sleep through a bout of sciatica. Thankfully, those nights are in the past.

One strategy that has helped me is to accept that I am awake for now. When you have done everything you can think of to improve your sleep and are still struggling, adopt a mindset of acceptance rather than getting into a dither over it. You will naturally be less agitated, which will paradoxically help you sleep better. Did you know there is evidence that some people do well sleeping two separate shifts per night? It is known as bimodal or biphasic sleep. Knowing this can make you feel a little better if you tend to wake up in the middle of the night.

Many of my clients like to read with dim lighting or amber, blue-blocking glasses. Others stay in bed and wait it out. If you wake up in the middle of the night, you may want to try deep breathing. Often, high cortisol levels can impact sleep, so mindfulness exercises that relax you can also be helpful.

🔑 TOC Example – Sleepy Moments

Technically, this is more of an example than a key, but I wanted to share this story. One client, Mary, had trouble sleeping and had undergone a sleep study, but the doctors told her she did not have sleep apnea. She was frustrated, exhausted, and in tears over her lack of sleep. Mary had a deadline looming at work and would ruminate about how little her teammates supported her. Her head was filled with worries over what was on her plate for the next day, and she became angrier and angrier the more sleep eluded her.

We worked together to develop a sleep plan until her new routine took hold. Mary implemented the following steps to improve her sleep, and within a week or two, she reported a major improvement.

1. The first thing Mary did was to start winding down for bed about an hour sooner. She dimmed her lights, avoided computer screens, and used blue-blocking glasses as necessary.

2. She also decided to implement a warm bath routine at night which would relax her muscles in preparation for bed.

3. While Mary's brain was a little too active at night for traditional meditation, she could use two or three of the non-meditation mindfulness techniques, trying out four-count box breathing, self-care-essing, neck massage, and TOC Talk.

4. Her TOC Talk included statements like: "This is a brief moment, it will pass. I am calm and relaxed, peaceful and content. Everything is going to be all right. Worrying about this is wasted energy."

5. When all else failed, Mary would read or listen to a podcast on her cell phone using the blue light blocking features and keeping the screen as dim as possible without causing eye strain.

Mary also adopted a mindset that it wasn't worth losing her peace of mind when she woke up for a short while. Eventually, she came to trust that she would always get back to sleep within a half hour, and that extra time she gained by getting set for bed a little earlier really made a difference.

One thing I do as part of my own TOC Sleep practice is express gratitude for my comfy bed and cozy blanket. I also use my pink sound machine continuously throughout the night and have invested in room-darkening shades and curtains. A friend of mine shared that she uses EFT, aka Tapping. For me, when sleep isn't perfect, my acceptance that I may be awake for a little while is what gets me through the night.

Final Thoughts

How you take care of your health, whether in the context of better nutrition, physical movement, safer care products, or sleep hygiene matters in your state of mind. It's not necessary to be perfect (I'm not) but paying attention to what your body needs can go a long way toward boosting your overall mood so you can truly become your best self and live a life filled with abundant joy and optimism. Next, I will guide you through assembling your own TOC Keys to create a personal optimism keychain. I will also share templates you can use to foster improvements in optimism levels based on specific challenges.

OPTIMISM DECODER

Chapter 9
Priming Your Body for a Healthier Mind
in an Insane World

- While there is not a one-size-fits-all eating plan, eating real unprocessed foods and avoiding 'fake foods' is key.

- Certain high-quality nutritional supplements may be a helpful addition for reducing stress and anxiety.

- There are toxins everywhere in this insane world, so do your best to limit exposure that can interfere with your health.

- Even though time may be limited, physical movement is important for boosting mood and alleviating stress.

- Be sure to get downtime and address any challenges you may have with getting sound sleep.

https://theoptimismcode.com

Chapter 10

Assembling Your Very Own Set of Optimism Keys

"Don't give up. Normally it is the last key on the ring which opens the door."

Paulo Coelho

You've made it far on your journey toward unlocking more optimism. Before we go any further, I want to congratulate you! Give yourself a pat on the back and a big smile. I am glad you persevered and am proud of you for arriving at this significant chapter.

Now that you have learned more about how the brain works, the value of gratitude, the importance of mindfulness, the benefits of positive self-talk, and more, it's time to put this knowledge into a realistic plan that fits your unique lifestyle.

In this chapter, you will build your own set of Optimism Keys to unlock more joy every day. I will guide you through the process, providing examples and suggestions to illustrate how to incorporate more positivity into your life. While reading this book is great, the magic of the Optimism Code lies in implementation.

Don't be discouraged and feel this isn't working when judgmental thoughts and the daily grind of living cause pessimism to creep in. This is normal; after all, you have a brain that is wired toward looking for threats, and you have been leaning toward negativity for a long time. To unlock your best self, your mission from here on out will be to realign your focus toward optimism continually. Don't berate yourself. Instead, grab your new set of keys and turn your attention toward the present.

As you develop more confidence and practice using your favorite Optimism Code techniques, your monkey mind will naturally learn your new routine, and pessimistic thinking will no longer grab hold of you the way it used to. It won't disappear, but it will shrink in significance over time. Let's review some core principles surrounding the habits you will form as you build your keychain.

Forming Habits—Dovetailing Routines

One of the best methods for forming any habit is to create what I like to call Dovetailing Routines. In the culinary arts, dovetailing refers to combining ingredients, particularly leftovers, in a new way so there's less waste and more efficiency. Funnily enough, I just did this yesterday. I usually cook a whole chicken a few times a month but prefer dark meat. My honey likes white meat, so I dovetail, using the leftovers to make him chicken salad.

Similarly, by strategically assembling a variety of different TOC Keys related to gratitude, mindfulness, self-talk, and health activities into specific sequences, your monkey mind will be trained, and you will naturally automate new, more positive thoughts and behavior patterns.

Just as a smoker forms a habit that includes reaching for the cigarette pack, getting the lighter, going outside during break time, inhaling, blowing smoke rings, and discarding the butt, you can string together a series of actions that are good for you too. When I stopped smoking many years ago, I was just as addicted to the process of smoking as I was to nicotine. I had to get used to not reaching for a cigarette after a meal, getting the ashtray and matches, etc.

I finally did it with acupuncture and odd tasting Asian herbs. I will never forget what the acupuncturist said to me: "For three days, you crave cigarette, and then, no more." She was right. I have noticed that three days is about the time it takes me to begin to automate my habits. It has been decades since I made the final move to become a non-smoker and I have never looked back. When putting together TOC Keys, we can use these same principles of new habit formation.

Multiple Key Rings

For those of you who have ever been in charge of the keys at your job or watched someone else's home while they were out of town, it's likely you have assembled a keychain that holds multiple key rings. Typically, each key ring will have a set of keys for use at the specific property you are entering. Similarly, you can think of dovetailing routines as key rings that take you to slightly different destinations on your larger optimism keychain. By arranging your TOC Keys in different assortments, you can create a variety of key rings and fire off a series of positive habits that your mind will automate.

We use this tendency of the brain all the time without even realizing it. In fact, it happened to me just this morning. I have a routine of drinking two small cups of iced coffee and have gotten into the habit of drinking a brand of iced green tea that is high in theanine for relaxation and low in lead. For a long time, it was my dovetailed beverage of choice immediately following my coffee.

Due to a stomach bug, I stopped this behavior for about a week and the habit link I'd formed was unintentionally broken. When I realized this, I re-created the habit by putting a cue (the teabag) in a place I would see near my coffee maker.

It took about three days to recreate a brain link after dovetailing my tea. Like magic, I once again started making a cup of green tea as soon as I finished my coffee. To add to my key ring, I automated a glass of ice water once the tea was done. Upon finishing the water, I linked a shower, followed by a brief meditation and then a walk.

TOC Key Ring: Morning Routine Example

To illustrate more clearly, the circle below is a key ring I have added to my own optimism keychain. These are my typical morning TOC Keys and are specific to me. They are based on my personal preferences, daily aches and pains, and time availability in the morning.

While you may choose to adopt some of them, other keys may not suit you at all. I have met many people who do not like baths, for example. Your TOC Key rings are unique, as no two people like exactly the same things.

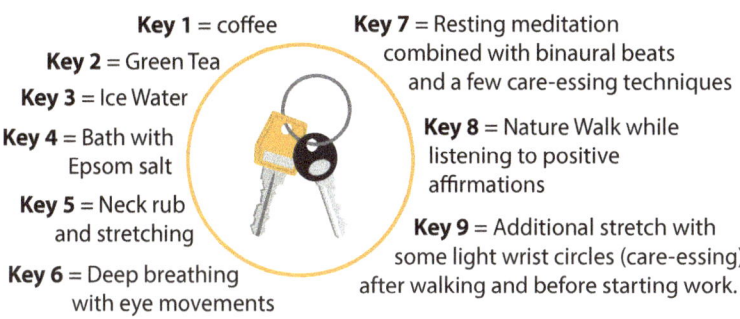

Key 1 = coffee

Key 2 = Green Tea

Key 3 = Ice Water

Key 4 = Bath with Epsom salt

Key 5 = Neck rub and stretching

Key 6 = Deep breathing with eye movements

Key 7 = Resting meditation combined with binaural beats and a few care-essing techniques

Key 8 = Nature Walk while listening to positive affirmations

Key 9 = Additional stretch with some light wrist circles (care-essing) after walking and before starting work.

On average, this particular key ring takes me anywhere from an hour to an hour and a half, but if I'm busy or have an appointment, I may limit my actions and modify my routine to accommodate my schedule, shrinking the process down. On days with more morning discomfort and more time, I may skip the walk and opt for longer meditation and stretching. My routine is automated, but as with computer programs, it resembles a flow chart based on day-to-day decision-making.

- What do I need?

- What can I eliminate in a pinch?

- What keys can I add to unlock even more joy today?

The great thing about creating a dovetailing routine is that it literally becomes wired in your brain. As if out of nowhere, you start to spontaneously think of the next key in the keychain.

Time Restraints

I am very fortunate that I don't have a commute or anyone depending on me in the morning. I recognize not everyone is so lucky. If you are in a position where you have to take care of others, it will be important for you to identify the best keys that will fit in with your morning routine based on a realistic assessment of the variables in your schedule. When I work with clients, we brainstorm and troubleshoot challenges together to assemble key rings that make sense on a case-by-case basis.

Creating Positivity One Key at a Time

While it may be tempting to focus on breaking old thinking patterns you don't want; I want you to aim your attention at filling your keychain with new strategies without worrying too much about your current thoughts. As you become more mindful, overriding your mind's natural slant toward negativity will get easier.

In the meantime, as you hear the monkey screeching, notice it while downplaying counterproductive thoughts. The voice in your head that feeds you negative thoughts has been there for a long time and is normal. Critical and upsetting thoughts should decrease over time but may never fully disappear, and that's okay. Once you decrease their importance and grab your keychain to combat them, it *will* get better.

Whenever I catch myself judging others or talking to myself about what is wrong instead of right, I quickly turn things around. I no longer beat myself up for having a stray negative thought. Instead, I troubleshoot to determine what I can do in the moment to create more joy going forward. It's so freeing!

Just the other day, I caught myself whining out loud over a torn muscle that is taking its sweet time to heal. I remembered to throw in a little humor and comedy. It is one of my go-to keys. Joking with myself, I thought about calling a whaaa-m-bulance. Thankfully, it was just a pulled muscle and nothing more serious. After a good laugh, I reminded myself, "Everything is gonna be all right."

Before I learned to use some of my TOC Keys effectively, I might have turned my "whaaa" into a full-blown self-pity party. Now, I just smiled at myself and rapidly took a secure viewpoint that my muscle would eventually heal. While life can dole out more serious issues than muscle strain, it is more common for the day-to-day stuff to get us down.

🔑 Angie's First Key Ring

One of my clients, Angie, works in an office and was struggling with a tremendous amount of overwhelm when we first met. She often felt like her spouse wasn't helping out enough with their three young children and pets. Understandably, creating a strategy to boost relaxation and alleviate her stress at home was not something she felt she could do at the beginning of our journey together. She ultimately decided the best time to run her dovetailing routine would be at work.

As Angie and I worked to uncover her current thoughts, habits, and behaviors, we were able to craft her first key ring. When Angie's monkey mind started screeching with resentment toward her husband, she would say things like, "This is all too much for me to handle. I can't deal with this right now," or "I'm going to lose my mind."

These thoughts undermined her self-worth. She felt she was falling short of perfection and *should* be able to keep up with it all. The things she was saying to herself were killing her joy and interfering with her marital happiness as well.

🔑 *Angie's TOC-Talk Key*

I asked Angie to formulate five TOC Talk statements to counterbalance her most common negative thoughts. She memorized these, so they became a habit, and she started using them in a dovetailed sequence, tying them to her commute and then using them throughout the day as stand-alone statements whenever she caught herself running her old scripts.

1. I can do it in bits and pieces.
2. I am capable of handling what comes my way.
3. You never fail until you stop trying.
4. I am an awesome human being.
5. Everything is going to be all right.

🔑 Angie's NMM Key

In addition to getting Angie up and running with TOC Talk, I worked with her to create a non-meditation mindfulness routine to calm her nerves during 15-minute work breaks or as a ritual at lunchtime. Angie began to implement a two-part TOC sequence that took less than five minutes but made a huge difference in her anxiety levels when coupled with her new self-talk.

The sequence went as follows:

1. **Breathe Deeply Just Once**

2. **Inhale** for 10 (nose), hold for 10, and exhale slowly for 10 (mouth), pause, breath normally.

3. **Tapping (EFT)**

   Angie had done tapping before and liked it but had stopped; I suggested that as soon as she was done with her daily breath, which she did in her office chair to signal the start of her break, she head to the ladies' room and do her tapping in private.

As Angie followed an EFT Tapping sequence she'd learned online, she silently said, "Even though I feel overwhelmed right now, I deeply and completely love and accept myself." She completed a few rounds until she felt she had a grip on her feelings.

Angie's Gratitude Key

After Angie was done tapping, she took a short break on the bench outside her building, weather permitting. Typically, she checked her phone or had lunch, depending on the time of day. Immediately following this, Angie dovetailed a short gratitude routine before returning to her desk. I recommended a gratitude app—all she had to do was quickly list three things for which she was grateful.

Because overwhelm was her core emotion, I suggested that the quickest method of practicing gratitude would be her best go-to. In a matter of seconds, Angie jotted down three things she was grateful for. It could be sunshine, air, and water, or it could be the love she has for her family, the job that pays her bills, or the new blouse she wore to work that led to lots of compliments from her peers.

Using a blend of unique self-talk, non-meditation mindfulness, and a short version of gratitude made a huge difference in Angie's outlook. She reported feeling more in control of her moods and started adding more optimism key rings throughout her day.

When she arrived home, Angie began spending intentional time walking and petting the dogs, savoring the experience rather than resenting it. In addition, she dovetailed a two to five-minute fun dance session with her children. The kids loved it, and it put them all in a fabulous mood, which set the tone for a positive evening. Her new routine was not only good for her but was good for the family, including her husband. Angie began to appreciate him more as they became a more cohesive team, sharing chores more evenly despite their busy schedules.

Angie's first TOC KEY RING

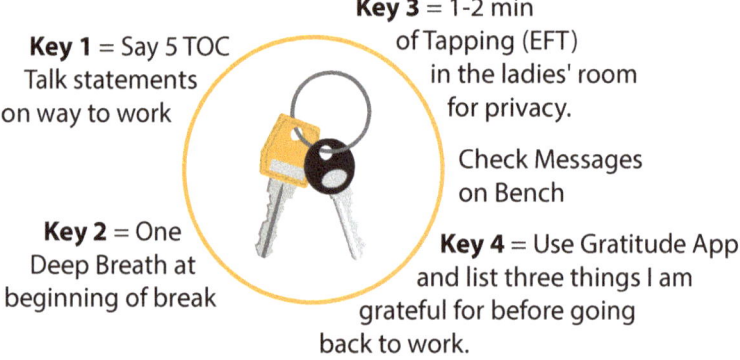

Key 1 = Say 5 TOC Talk statements on way to work

Key 3 = 1-2 min of Tapping (EFT) in the ladies' room for privacy.

Check Messages on Bench

Key 2 = One Deep Breath at beginning of break

Key 4 = Use Gratitude App and list three things I am grateful for before going back to work.

Building Your Own Set of Keys

Now that I've provided a couple of examples for assembling key rings on your optimism keychain, I want to review the various keys available to you. We have covered a lot, and I recognize it can be a little bit confusing. For this reason, I am including a list of the strategies we've covered.

Choose five keys to start and build from there. You can create just one key ring with your selections or put one or two keys on several keychains you activate at different times of the day. The choice is yours. Even though I recommend you start with five keys, if you are already using some of these techniques and feel you can manage more, go for it.

As you add different keys to your key rings, don't be afraid to remove a few keys as well. Take what works and use it. Discard the keys that don't quite feel right to you. Or, save them for a future time when they might work better. Think of your building process as an experimentation phase. You can't do anything wrong and there are no mistakes. Play with this as if you were an artist trying out new colors to see which ones you like best. The only way to get no benefit is to do nothing.

I have sorted this as best I can so you can pick and choose from the lists, but there is some overlap from one category to the next. For example, a gratitude phrase can also be used as a positive TOC Talk statement. You can also make up your own sayings based on what feels right to you. Spin toward where you want to be rather than away from where you don't, and you can't get it wrong. Keep your attention on how you feel after using any individual key. You are one of a kind, and while I wish I could wave a magic wand and tell you precisely which keys will work for you, I can't.

Even my coaching clients need to do some soul-searching (with my guidance, of course) to figure out what works when unlocking their own Optimism Code. As you pick and choose from the lists below, think about the "Good, Better, Best" approach based on your schedule and motivation level. Luckily, most of the keys take up very little time, and some of them can be done in seconds.

Choose Your First Keys

GRATITUDE

I'm grateful for:

The little things (pleasures) found in daily life, like petting a cute dog or looking at beautiful flowers. Other things I am grateful for include indoor plumbing in the middle of the night and my hands working as I'm typing this book and sharing some of the optimism keys with you.

Now you:

What are three things off the top of your head that you are grateful for today?

🔑 1._____

🔑 2._____

🔑 3._____

Do you have shelter? Is there air for you to breathe? Have you eaten today? Do you have access to clean water? What else makes you feel grateful in this moment and why?

MINDFULNESS

I want to recap the various non-meditation mindfulness (NMM) techniques and the options you have available for regular meditation. We have covered a lot of ground. This is a marathon, not a sprint, so select one or two techniques you feel you can manage and practice that Optimism Key before adding more to your keychain.

🔑 Consider practicing the Sunshine Gaze or Hot Shower Mindfulness exercises in addition to the choices below. Don't forget about the Positive What-iffing technique when you catch yourself ruminating and conjuring up fearful, negative thoughts about the future.

Non-Meditation Mindfulness (NMM)

Breathing Techniques

🔑 Slow and Long, Box Breathing, Triangle Breathing, Meditative Breathing, or Listen and Do Nothing (See Chapter 4 for specific instructions.)

Song and Dance

🔑 Listen to your favorite songs and sing along loudly or dance to the beat.

🔑 Enjoy singing bowls, binaural beats, or hang/tongue drum music.

Relieve Tense Muscles

Conduct an NMM Body Scan or try the Quick-Fix Relaxation Response (See Chapter 5 for instructions.) You can also do self-massage, which is particularly helpful at the base of the neck and around the shoulders. Feel around for pressure points to release feel-good endorphins.

The Eyes Have It

🔑 Consider trying the Eye Rolling technique to bring focus to the front of your brain or try covering your eyes with your palms (as described in Chapter 5). You can even sit and stare at a candle or a fireplace if you are lucky enough to have one.

Care-essing

While they might seem a little weird, the care-essing techniques are great for improving mood. If you are in the presence of others, I recommend the Easy Hand Care-ess. I also like the wrist and arm version of care-essing if you want to release oxytocin, also known as the love hormone. Facial care-essing is the best, and you would be amazed at how you can do a simple care-ess in public, and no one will even notice. If you haven't tried any of the care-essing techniques, put it on your list as a great addition to your key rings for use now or in the future.

🔑 Easy Hand Care-ess

🔑 Wrist and Arm Care-essing

🔑 Facial Care-essing

Tapping - EFT

I am not the Tapping guru as others with much greater expertise can provide more insight on benefits and techniques related to this Emotional Freedom Technique. You can certainly put EFT on your optimism keychain as a great tool to boost positivity rapidly.

Journaling

Unlike many other self-help books, I have not focused much on journaling. While I have gone through phases of journaling a lot and know many who benefit from it, I prefer to focus on a few other Optimism Keys. That said, I appreciate the value of journaling, especially if you enjoy it and can be consistent with it. My only caveat is that if you tend to write down a lot of negative things, I invite you to counterbalance those with positivity as well.

Additional NMM mind-body hacks and stress-reduction techniques include using essential oils, viewing images of nature and animals, hot and cold therapy, compassion meditation (Kristin Neff), self-reiki, yoga, and stretching.

Meditation Options

Here is a list of the many varieties of meditation you may want to explore. While I am a big fan of meditation, it isn't for everyone. That said, once you use other methods to calm your mind, you may find your experience with meditating becomes easier and more enjoyable.

🔑 Guided Meditation

🔑 Visualization

🔑 Mindfulness Based
   Stress Reduction (MBSR)

🔑 Dr. Joe Dispenza Meditation

🔑 Chakra Meditation

🔑 Mantra Meditation

🔑 Yoga-Nidra | iRest

🔑 Walking Meditation

These and other forms of meditation can effectively calm the mind, boost positivity, and train your brain to center itself back on the present. Whether you use an app, listen to a podcast, or purchase a recording, meditation is amazing for managing stress and anxiety. You can start with one to five minutes and build from there.

Which meditation options do you think you may want to try first?

_____

_____

BODY AND BRAIN HEALTH

These five keys will go a long way toward improving your brain health.

- 🔑 Eat real food and limit snacking
- 🔑 Consider Brain Power supplements
- 🔑 Select home and personal care products wisely.
- 🔑 Develop a movement and physical activity plan.
- 🔑 Address any sleep issues you may have as best you can.

Which keys do you want to use to improve your body and brain health?

_____

_____

TOC TALK, AFFIRMATIONS, & RE-FRAMERS

I want you to think about what you can say to yourself that would boost your joy or help you cope with any upsetting thoughts or daily events.

Here are a few of mine today:

🔑 *Slogan:* I can do things in bits and pieces (to complete this book.)

🔑 *Cliché:* "To know even one life has breathed easier because you have lived, this is to have succeeded." This is a quote from Ralph Waldo Emerson. It's one of my favorites and worth repeating.

🔑 *Affirmation:* I am strong and capable.

🔑 *Re-framer:* Even though I feel tired and my body aches more than usual today, I am doing what needs to get done in the here and now, which is a huge positive.

Other TOC Talk phrases you might consider are below. You can change the verb tense of these depending upon how saying them makes you feel. You can even change the wording to customize them to your own way of thinking and speaking. Feel free to read them, write them down, and even record them for yourself to memorize. The bracketed parts are for your understanding and don't necessarily need to be said. In my view, shorter is sweeter for ease of memorization, but trust your instincts.

Note: There are many slogans. They are listed for you in no particular order and have been broken into groups of five to make reviewing them easier.

Affirmations ("I am" statements)

These are self-esteem-boosting affirmations, but you can make any affirmation you want to, so phrases like, "I am a non-smoker," and "I am a healthy eater," for example, can be used to transform bad habits. The sky's the limit when it comes to positive affirmations. As mentioned previously, there are online videos and audio you can use as well, which I do frequently.

🔑 I am a beautiful person.

🔑 I am worthy and loved.

🔑 I am important to the world.

🔑 I am valuable and needed.

🔑 I am an awesome human being.

For things you don't fully believe, you can state, "I am becoming…" or "I am getting…".

🔑 I am getting better and becoming an amazing person day by day.

🔑 I am becoming healthy and fit in each and every moment.

One of my favorites, which I often say, is, "I am reverse aging." It helps me focus on taking the necessary steps to improve my health daily.

Can you think of one or two "I am" affirmations you can use right now that will motivate you?

_____

_____

Slogans

🔑 My beliefs are not necessarily true (not everyone sees the world in the same way).

I'm just human. I'm stronger than I think (even when I am imperfect).

It's a minor nuisance (not big of a deal).

It's the little things (in life that bring me joy).

Anyone in my shoes might feel the same way.

🔑 Being imperfect is okay. (Nobody else is perfect either.)

There is nothing wrong with me (that isn't wrong with everyone else).

If I change my focus, my feelings will follow.

I can do things in bits and pieces (so I don't get overwhelmed).

Moods vary like the tide. (We all have highs and lows.)

🔑 It's not worth losing my peace of mind over (or making myself sick).

We can't always be on the same wavelength (as one another).

When we can't change the world, we can change our response.

Worrying about this is wasted energy (that could be put to better use).

It's a brief moment. (You'll get over it and feel better in time.)

🔑 Give yourself a pat on the back (for your efforts).

You can change your mood by moving your body.

Use humor and comedy (to make yourself feel better).

You can only control your inner self, not the outer world.

You have a right to feel this way (without guilt).

Clichés:

🔑 You never fail until you stop trying.

🔑 This too shall pass.

🔑 Whatever doesn't kill you makes you stronger.

🔑 There is a solution to every problem.

What other clichés can you think of that resonate with you?

_____

Re-framers

Remember the story I told about my neighbor who has a habit of leaving his door ajar and how I made up a story? If a situation in your life has been bothering you, try to think of how you might reframe it. What could you say to yourself that would bring you more peace of mind? Many of the TOC Talk statements can help you develop alternative stories to help you reframe negative situations and feel better. As I mentioned in Chapter 6, your re-framers don't necessarily have to be true to be effective.

Is there anything happening in your life right now that you could reframe in a more positive light? If so, jot it down.

 _____

ENJOY THE PROCESS

When we began this journey, I desired to give you a wide variety of tools and techniques to transform your stress and anxiety into optimism and joy. I truly want you to become your best self and I want you to enjoy the process.

Your personal optimism keychain doesn't need to be big and bulky. Selecting your Optimism Keys can be fun and should be approached in a lighthearted, exploratory way. When I wear my career coaching hat, I often tell job seekers to approach job search as a networking exercise rather than a chore. I feel the same way about building key rings. While it may seem like a lot of work because there are so many keys available, each key is simplistic and can be implemented in seconds or minutes. If one key doesn't work, try another. Just as a job seeker goes on more than one interview, the optimism seeker must try multiple strategies based on personal preference and trial and error.

Take Action

Doing what you can when you can is the best way to prevent overwhelm when building your optimism keychain. If you have more time on the weekend, create a weekend-only optimism key ring. The important thing is to move forward toward optimism every day, even when your resilience is tested. Keep going, and you will get there.

You have been programmed to think a certain way for a very long time. While you can implement many keys immediately, other keys may take longer to become an integral part of your new, more optimistic mind. I encourage you to make a basic list of the possible keys you want to use both in the short term and long term. There may be some overlap, but that is okay. The important thing is to make a plan, break it down into small, doable steps, and, above all else, take action. Nothing happens if nothing happens.

Short Term Keys

_____

_____

_____

_____

_____

_____

Long Term Keys

_____

_____

_____

_____

_____

_____

While building your new optimism keychain, do not become discouraged if old habits and thinking patterns persist. Old automations take time to reprogram. As a perfect example, I recently moved to a new home. During the move, I packed up my belongings, and some of my items were in different places than usual. Yet my mind, on autopilot, would constantly run scripts as if everything was still in the same location. I found myself opening empty drawers and reaching for objects no longer in their place. I consciously knew they had been moved, but my monkey mind kept doing its thing.

Even while I was writing this book and creating The Optimism Code website, I found myself battling worrisome thoughts and feelings, particularly when the process didn't go as smoothly as I would have liked. The good news is that I used my own set of Optimism Keys, and they worked! My peace of mind grew stronger while my productivity soared despite the challenges I faced along the way. This is what I wish for you, too.

At the end of this book, I have included a link to various resources, including access to The Optimism Code blog, to help you take things to the next level. I am optimistic (of course) that this is just the beginning and not the end of our journey together!

OPTIMISM DECODER

Chapter 10
Assembling Your Very Own Set of Optimism Keys

- When negative thoughts come along, you can refocus your attention on one of the many Optimism Keys.

- Using "Dovetailing Routines" can help you build habits and create "Optimism Key Rings" for your Optimism Keychain.

- Consider your time restraints and personal situations as you select the keys that you are most drawn to.

- Emphasize building new habits rather than breaking old patterns.

- You can choose from a wide variety of keys to build your keychain, starting with just a few and building from there.

- While this book is nearing its end, your journey is just beginning towards a life filled with greater peace-of-mind.

- Learning from a book is great, but in order to benefit, it is important to implement and take action.

https://theoptimismcode.com

Resources

**"Optimism is a journey towards joy
best taken moment by moment."**
Wendy J. Schwartz

One of the main reasons I wrote *The Optimism Code: Grab the Keys to Unlock Your Best Self* is to share the many things that have helped me over the years as a person with emotional sensitivity. In my own journey to find ways of reducing my stress and anxiety, I took the best elements of what I read and implemented them.

I want you to do the same, so I have assembled a list of my favorite resources, including books, videos, podcasts, apps, programs, and products, to help you find what works for you. Not everything works for everyone, so I want you to have access to a variety of resources. Experiment and decide what resonates with you.

Since the resources I recommend are ever-changing, and someday I may pass the baton to the next generation of Optimism Code leaders, I felt it best to put this information directly on The Optimism Code website: https://theoptimismcode.com

SPREAD THE WORD

If you enjoyed this book, please tell others about The Optimism Code. You can scan the QR code or enter the

URL in any browser to get to the website. Also, if you liked this book, please remember to leave a review wherever you purchased it.

Thank you. I am grateful and anticipate good things for you—with optimism!

https://theoptimismcode.com

www.ingramcontent.com/pod-product-compliance
Lightning Source LLC
Chambersburg PA
CBHW050447150626
46551CB00029B/1944